ENGLISH # HERITAGE

Book of
Roman Bath

Barry Cunliffe

Deae Svli Minervae
D.D.

ENGLISH ✠ HERITAGE

Book of
Roman
Bath

Barry Cunliffe

B. T. Batsford / English Heritage
London

© B. Cunliffe 1995

First published as *Roman Bath Discovered*
1971 by Routledge & Kegan Paul plc. 1995

Second revised edition 1984
This edition is modified and updated

Typeset by Bernard Cavender Design & Greenwood Graphics Publishing
Printed and bound in Great Britain by
The Bath Press, Bath

Published by B.T. Batsford Ltd
4 Fitzhardinge Street, London W1H 0AH

A CIP catalogue record for this book is
available from the British Library

ISBN 0 7134 7892 6 (cased)
0 7134 7893 4 (limp)

Contents

Illustrations

Colour plates

Acknowledgements

The illustrations for this book, unless otherwise stated, have been prepared over the years by my colleagues at the Institute of Archaeology, University of Oxford. The original artwork for the line drawings is substantially the work of Alison Wilkins while the photographs have been prepared by, or under the direction of, Bob Wilkins. The exceptions are nos **30**, **34** and **73** which were drawn for the Bath Archaeological Trust by Miss Sheila Gibson, **colour plates 4, 11** and **12** which were drawn by John Ronayne also for the Bath Archaeological Trust, and nos **27, 32** and **35** which were drawn by the author. The photograph for **colour plate 6** was kindly provided by the Bath Archaeological Trust. I am most grateful to all those concerned and also to Mrs Lynda Smithson for typing the text with her customary attention to detail.

My colleagues in Bath, Sam Hunt and Stephen Bird, successively Directors of the Museums Service, and Pete Davenport, Director of the Bath Archaeological Trust, have been a welcome source of encouragement and advice.

Preface

My first visit to Bath, forty years ago, was as a schoolboy setting out with two friends on a walking tour of the West Country. The miracle of the preservation of the Roman buildings, buried so deep beneath the modern city, and the awareness of how much there was still to discover, made a deep impression – an impression enhanced, no doubt, by the fact that that day was the first occasion I had broken free from the constraints of the home environment to explore the world (albeit a rather restricted corner of it!). Eight years later, in 1963, I returned to the West Country, to a teaching post at Bristol University, at the same time becoming director of the newly formed Bath Excavation Committee. Since then I have maintained a constant involvement in the city and its archaeology. It has been a long and happy association.

The work of the Bath Excavation Committee and its successor body, the Bath Archaeological Trust, has, over the last thirty years, transformed our understanding of the Roman sanctuary and its setting. Most of the new information obtained during that period is now readily accessible in a series of detailed specialist reports. But even more satisfying has been the way in which the city's Museums Service, working closely with the Trust, has been able greatly to extend the area of the Roman centre available for visitors to see,

and has made it all the more accessible through modern displays and attractive guidebooks.

The original version of this book, under the title of *Roman Bath Discovered*, was first published in 1971 and was revised and updated for a second edition which appeared in 1984. The present edition has been updated and expanded to take note of new discoveries made over the last decade but, to keep within the length of the English Heritage series, the three chapters dealing with the beginnings of antiquarian interest and the discovery of the baths and the temple have been reduced in content and conflated into a single account. The guide to antiquarian writings about Roman Bath has also been omitted. For this reason the book has been retitled *Roman Bath*.

The discovery of Roman Bath is a continuous process but one of fits and starts. The period 1979–86 was a time of great activity leading to major new discoveries. The last decade has been quieter but at any moment redevelopment, however limited in scale, may produce surprises. After all it was the digging of a sewer trench which, on 12 July 1727, presented to the world the spectacular gilded bronze head of the goddess Minerva.

Barry Cunliffe
Oxford
January 1995

1
The setting

Bath nestles in a bend of the River Avon protected on all sides by the steep limestone scarp of the southern Cotswolds through which the river has scored its course (**1**). In prehistoric times the Cotswold ridge provided a natural corridor of communication. The river offered another. Bath lay at the crossing point protected, successively, by the Iron Age hill-forts of Bathampton and Little Solsbury. But the site, later to become the Roman sanctuary and settlement of Aquae Sulis, had other attractions. Within the compass of 100 metres (328ft) of each other three natural springs broke through the surface of the Lias clay, here outcropping from beneath the limestone mantle. The constant flow of mineral water was hot – 49°C at the Hot Bath spring, 46°C at the King's Bath and 40°C at the Cross Bath. The most copious was the King's Bath spring with the flow of nearly a third of a million gallons a day.

The spring water which bubbles up today is very old. It fell as rain 6000 years or more ago on the Mendip Hills and sank down deep into the rock, flowing along the bedding planes and fissures of the carboniferous limestone which here was contorted into a deep syncline – a basin shape, the Mendips forming one exposed rim (**2**). Some 3000–4000m (9800–13,000ft) down the water was heated to between 60 and 90°C by the earth's natural heat and under pressure rose again along a fault line – the Penny Quick fault – to emerge at Bath, cooled a little on its journey of return but still a forceful torrent. So it has been for at least 10,000 years.

To clear Bath, in the mind, of its rich overlay of buildings and to imagine what the scene was like 2000 years ago is not easy. The springs emerged on a promontory of land, thrust out from the limestone upland of Lansdown, protected on three sides by the fast-flowing river (**3**). The promontory seems to have been composed of two low knolls rising a few metres above the flood plain. The Cross Bath and Hot Bath springs rose towards the crest of the western knoll, their joint outfall flowing south-westwards to the river, while the far more powerful King's Bath spring rose between the two hillocks, its more violent flow creating the valley between them.

The river snaked across a wide flood plain up to 200m (656ft) across. Marshy, braided with small streams and choked with vegetation, it would have formed a formidable barrier except to those who knew the more solid ground and the fords. Of all the possible crossings the best would probably have been just to the north-east of the old city between the present Pulteney and Cleveland Bridges, for here the valley is considerably narrowed by a rise of drier ground in the valley floor to the east of the river. The ford, just south of Cleveland Bridge, is likely to have provided a major crossing in the early Roman period, as we will see.

To see the hot steamy water gush out of the opening in the side of the Roman reservoir today is an awe-inspiring sight. How much more dramatic would the flow of water have been in the natural surroundings of 2000 years ago, the vivid orange-red of the iron salts violent and unsettling

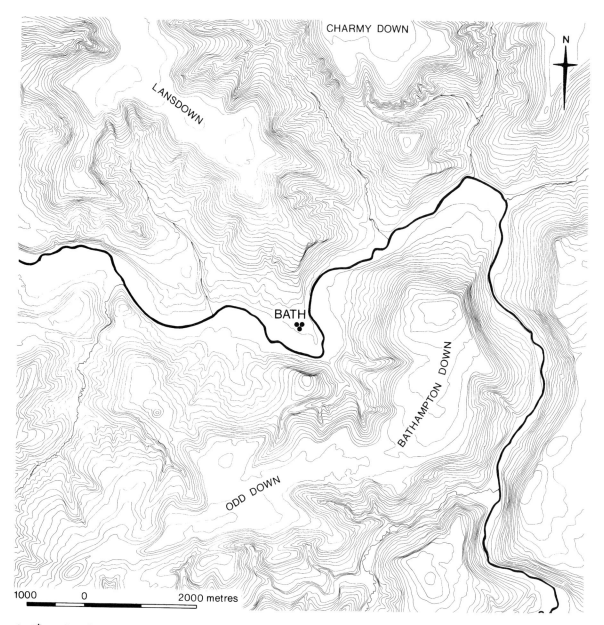

1 *The valley of the Avon cuts through the Cotswolds creating a steep-sided valley. Bath commands one of the most convenient crossing places.*

against the natural greens and greys, the whole scene made more frightening by the uncertain movements of the hovering steam. Little wonder that the place was thought to belong to the gods.

The early prehistory of the Bath region is not well known, though the evidence at present available suggests that occupation was quite dense.

Mesolithic hunters camped among the hot springs while Neolithic and Bronze Age structures cluttered the neighbouring hills. Iron Age settlements are better known. A large Early Iron Age hilltop enclosure dominates Bathampton Hill, while on the opposite side of the river, on the hill of Little Solsbury, a more strongly defended site was built probably in the fifth century BC and occupied for several centuries. Little is known of occupation on the site of Bath at this time. A settlement of some kind existed a little to the north at Sion Hill, while

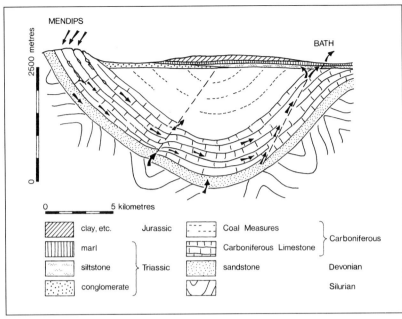

2 *Rain falling on the Mendips eventually emerges 8000 or more years later at Bath having been heated by the earth's natural internal heat.*

3 *The springs of Bath emerge on a low spur surrounded on three sides by the flood plain of the River Avon.*

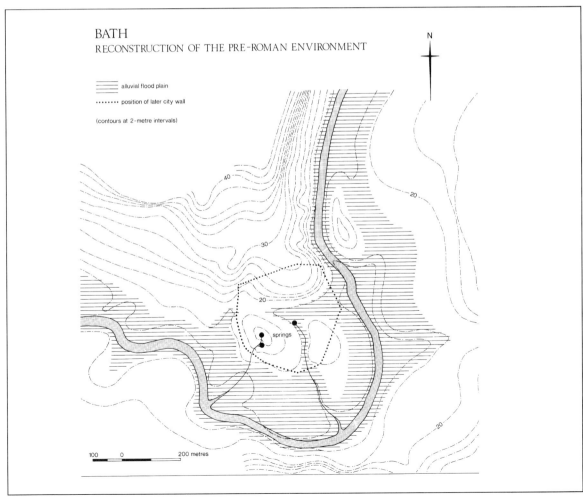

BATH
RECONSTRUCTION OF THE PRE-ROMAN ENVIRONMENT

alluvial flood plain

position of later city wall

(contours at 2-metre intervals)

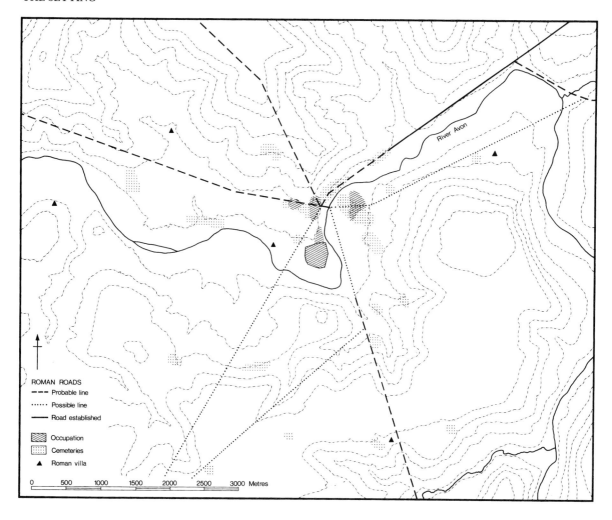

ROMAN ROADS
- - - Probable line
.... Possible line
——— Road established

▨ Occupation
▦ Cemeteries
▲ Roman villa

0 500 1000 1500 2000 2500 3000 Metres

4 *The Roman roads appear to converge on a crossing three-quarters of a kilometre north of the sanctuary. The details of the road system are not, however, well known.*

some 3km (2 miles) to the north-west, at Weston, two bronze spoons, probably a ritual deposit, were recovered from a spring in 1864.

Around the springs themselves Roman and later building has destroyed or obscured traces of earlier activity but during the excavation of the King's Bath spring we found evidence of a rubble and gravel causeway, pre-dating the Roman reservoir, which had been built out towards the centre of the spring. It had been edged with small stakes to stop the spring eroding it. Presumably it was along here the suppliants made their way through the alder swamp which surrounded the spring, to the point where the hot water bubbled up, there to view the most sacred spot and make their offerings to Sulis, goddess of the spring. Two thousand years later a few of these offerings – 18 Celtic coins – were

recovered when once more the causeway was uncovered and the mud of the spring excavated.

It was probably by the autumn of AD 43 that the Roman army, under Aulus Plautius, began laying out the first Roman frontier in Britain, choosing the Jurassic ridge as the line of the main military communication axis, later to become known as the Fosseway, slicing across the island from Lyme Bay to the Humber. The road, strung along with forts, provided the anchor for a military zone extending to the rivers Severn and Trent.

The Fosseway crossed the River Avon at Bath. The Avon crossing was important, not only for the

Fosseway but because here converged the west road leading from London, through Silchester and Mildenhall to the port of Sea Mills (*Abonae*) at Avonmouth and the south-east road across Wessex to the southern port at Hamworthy on Poole Harbour. Bath was a strategic route node of some importance. As our map (**4**) shows, the exact lines of the roads in the vicinity of the settlement are not well known but it is reasonably certain that the ford at Cleveland Bridge provided the principal crossing point, though the existence of another, to the south-west of the town, is a strong possibility.

Where the fort guarding the crossing was sited it is impossible yet to say. The most likely site would be just to the north-west of the later walled area in the vicinity of Queen's Square. Another possibility is to the east of the river at Bathwick. No doubt the issue will be one day resolved. Here it is sufficient to acknowledge that the importance of the river-crossing saw the Roman army firmly established on the site of Bath by the winter of AD 43. How, over the next few generations, they and their successors were to respond to the remarkable phenomenon of the hot springs and the native goddess who presided over them, provides the focus of this book. But first let us briefly consider how Roman Bath has been gradually brought to light.

2
The discovery of Roman Bath

The awareness of Bath's importance in the Roman past has never really been lost. The first reference to the springs and the temple is given by the Roman writer Solinus who, in the early third century, published *Collectanea rerum memorabilium* – a description of notable phenomena pieced together from hearsay and observation, covering the whole of the Roman empire. Writing of Britain, he says that there were hot springs 'furnished luxuriously for human use', and 'over these springs Minerva presides and in her temple the perpetual fire never whitens to ash, but as the flame fades, turns into rocky lumps'. There can be very little doubt that he is writing about Bath. The hot springs were famous throughout the Roman world, indeed the second-century geographer Ptolemy calls Bath *Aquae Calidae*. The mention of the temple fire is of particular interest for Solinus is almost certainly referring to the use of Somerset coal, a suggestion given substance by the discovery of a heap of cinders in the corner of the temple precinct in 1867.

Knowledge of the temple's existence, deriving presumably from the work of Solinus, is next made explicit in the legendary history of the kings of Britain – *Historia Regum Britanniae* – compiled by a Welsh cleric, Geoffrey of Monmouth, some time about AD 1135. He says that Bladud, father of King Lear, founded Bath and constructed its hot baths. He lit fires in the temple of Minerva, whom he had chosen as the goddess of the baths. A legend of unknown origin says that Bladud contracted leprosy while travelling abroad and

returned to live in voluntary exile near Bath. One day, while meditating on a hill overlooking Bath, he noticed that his pigs had suddenly rushed down into an alder swamp below, where they began to wallow in the black mud around a spring. It occurred to him that this was an odd thing even for pigs to do in winter, but as he approached he saw that the spring was hot and concluded that the pigs came to enjoy the warm mud. He soon noticed, however, that the mud bath had cured the animals of the sores and scurf from which they had been suffering. Being of an enquiring mind, he decided to see what effect the mud would have on his leprosy: needless to say, he was cured. He eventually returned to his father's court and when, some years later, he succeeded to the throne, he showed his gratitude by building the baths around the spring at Bath.

The story continued to be told with modifications and amendments. One version tells how Bladud built a magnificent city around the baths and lived there into his declining years, until one day he finally succumbed to his delusions of grandeur and decided to fly from the top of Minerva's Temple, with a notable, and fatal, lack of success. The Bladud story provides a splendid origin myth for Bath. Whether it is more than that we will never know.

It is to John Leland, librarian, chaplain and, later, antiquary to Henry VIII, that we owe the first description of the physical remains of Roman Bath. Between 1536 and 1542 Leland travelled the length and breadth of Britain. It was the time of the Dissolution when monastery libraries were being broken up and the manuscripts dispersed. It was also a time of renewed interest in the past when, after a long period of arid speculation, it was realised that new information accessible only to those prepared to travel and observe was desperately needed. When Leland arrived at Bath he began to study its monuments and buildings in some detail. He describes the gates and the circuit of the wall 'of no great highth', and notes that no towers survived except at the gates themselves. Then follows an admirable description of carved stones, presumably of Roman date, embedded in the superstructure of the wall:

> There be divers notable antiquitees engravid in stone that yet be sene yn the walles of Bathe betweixt the south gate and the weste gate: and agayn betwixt the west gate and the north gate. The first was an antique hed of a man made al flat and having great lokkes of here as I have in a coine of C. Antius. The secunde that I did se bytwene the south and the north gate was an image, as I tooke it, of Hercules: for he held yn eche hand a serpent.

The description is quite remarkable for its accuracy and perception. Yet Leland was not content simply to record his observations. He offered some comment on them, arguing that the blocks were more likely to be reused in post-Roman rebuilding than set in place in the Roman period. He is the first scholar to offer any record of the antiquities which, though noted on subsequent occasions, gradually disappeared as the wall was pulled down piece by piece to make way for new developments.

Leland settled down in 1545 to begin to prepare his voluminous notes for publication, but five years later he was certified insane and in 1552 he died, his work unfinished. The notes eventually found their way into the Bodleian Library at Oxford, where they were used freely by those who followed in Leland's footsteps, men such as the equally famous topographer William

Camden (died 1765), but it was not until 1710–12 that *The Itinerary of John Leland* was eventually published under the editorship of Thomas Hearne. Leland's travels had, however, initiated a new era in antiquarian studies. William Camden, Thomas Guidott (end seventeenth century) and William Stukeley (died 1765) all visited Bath and noted further Roman stones. Camden, for example, was able to record two newly discovered tombstones, found in 1592 at Walcot on the line of the Roman Fosseway, in a late edition of his *Britannia*. These important inscriptions, like so much seen in the sixteenth and seventeenth centuries, have since disappeared.

Throughout the sixteenth and seventeenth centuries knowledge of the curative thermal waters of Bath spread, attracting to the city an unceasing flow of visitors, even though the facilities left something to be desired. The architect John Wood the elder, who began to transform the city in 1725, provides a somewhat unalluring description of the baths as he first saw them. They were, he said, 'like so many bear gardens; and modesty was entirely shut out of them; people of both sexes bathing by day and night naked; and dogs, cats, and pigs, even human creatures, were hurl'd over the rails into the water, while people were bathing in it'.

Nevertheless the growing fame of the waters brought illustrious visitors prepared to face these horrors. In Charles I's reign, Queen Henrietta Maria preferred the English springs to those of her native France. Catherine of Braganza, Mary of Modena, Anne of Denmark, they all came, but it was the visit of Princess Anne in 1692 and her return as queen ten years later that provided the final impetus to the town and flung it suddenly to the forefront of genteel acceptability.

The eighteenth century saw Bath transformed and with this transformation came a spate of remarkable archaeological discoveries. The first, and in many ways the most remarkable of all, came in 1727 when a deep sewer trench was being dug along Stall Street. On 12 July, in the mud and rubble at the bottom of the trench, a workman came upon a life-sized gilded bronze

5 *Life-size gilded bronze head of the goddess Minerva found during the digging of a sewer beneath Stall Street in 1727. The head was once crowned with a separate Corinthian helmet and the entire figure would probably have been the cult statue of the temple.*

head of Minerva, which at some time in the past had been broken from the torso and discarded. The head (**5, colour plate 1**) is a fine piece of competent, if somewhat dull, Roman workmanship, showing Minerva with her hair parted in the middle. The unfinished top to her head suggests that she was originally wearing a detachable Corinthian helmet. There can be no doubt that the statue to which the head belonged would have been of very considerable importance in Roman Bath – it might well have been the cult statue from the temple itself, but of this we can never be sure. A month later, in the same sewer trench, a hypocaust of the baths was briefly uncovered. It was a dramatic beginning but other discoveries were soon to follow. In 1738 John Wood, digging the foundations for The Mineral Water Hospital, just inside the north wall of the town, uncovered part of a Roman building complete with hypocausts and mosaics.

The next discovery was altogether more spectacular. In 1755 work began on the construction of a suite of baths, called the Duke of Kingston's Baths, over the site of the west range of the abbey claustral buildings, at this date known as the Abbot's House. The softness of the ground hereabouts demanded deep footings, and it is hardly surprising that, immediately the soil removal began, archaeological details started to emerge: first the remains of a Saxon cemetery and later most of what is now known to be the east end of the Roman bathing establishment, excellently preserved. Such a staggering discovery naturally attracted widespread interest. The work was closely watched and recorded by Dr Charles Lucas with the help of John Wood, the architect, and an account was published in his *Essays on the Waters* in 1756; but the fullest description was provided by the artist William Hoare, then resident in Bath. In 1762 he sent a plan and perspective of the excavations (**6**), together with a covering letter to a now unknown member of the aristocracy describing the Roman structures in considerable detail. The discoveries of 1727 and 1755 had, in fact, defined the west and east extremities of the thermal bathing establishment.

The growing popularity and increasing affluence of the spa led the civic authorities to engage in a policy of extensive rebuilding. By 1790 they had decided that the Pump Room, built in 1706 and enlarged in 1751, needed replacement. Thomas Baldwin was appointed to supervise the

work and, by the autumn, foundation trenches for the north and west walls had been sunk into the mud and rubble to a depth of 4m (13ft), at which a solid Roman pavement was discovered, while the earth above was found to be packed with collapsed Roman masonry. More than seventy blocks of sculpted and inscribed stone were recovered. Several contemporary accounts were published but all the early work was surpassed when, in 1813, Samuel Lysons produced his first volume of *Reliquiae Britannico-Romanae* – a brilliantly illustrated and highly accurate description of each of the carved and inscribed stones (**7**, **8**). Lysons's book is still a standard work, particularly as several of the stones mentioned have since been lost. Nor was he satisfied simply to describe what he saw. He also offered a reasoned reconstruction of some of the monuments, showing, for example, that many of the fragments belonged to the main front elevation of a remarkable Corinthian temple, the pediment of which depicted a glowering Gorgon's head – this was, without any doubt, the Temple of Minerva.

The discoveries of 1790 had shown two things: that the temple lay somewhere to the north or west of the spring in the region of the Pump Room, and that it was in style a purely Classical composition worthy of a place in Rome. Yet there was a distinctly local flavour about its pediment: the Gorgon, in Classical mythology always female, was depicted here as a male and a Celtic male at that. What Baldwin's labourers had uncovered was a perfect example of the conflation between a Roman and native deity. The Roman half was Minerva, the local component was the goddess Sulis mentioned many times on inscriptions found in various parts of the town. Thenceforth the temple must be ascribed to Sulis Minerva. Its discovery was a fitting end to the century which had witnessed the city's transformation.

The first sixty years of the nineteenth century saw little significant building activity in the centre of Bath. The construction of York Street in 1803 brought to light a few fragments of masonry belonging to the south side of the Great Bath, while a small part of the west baths was briefly

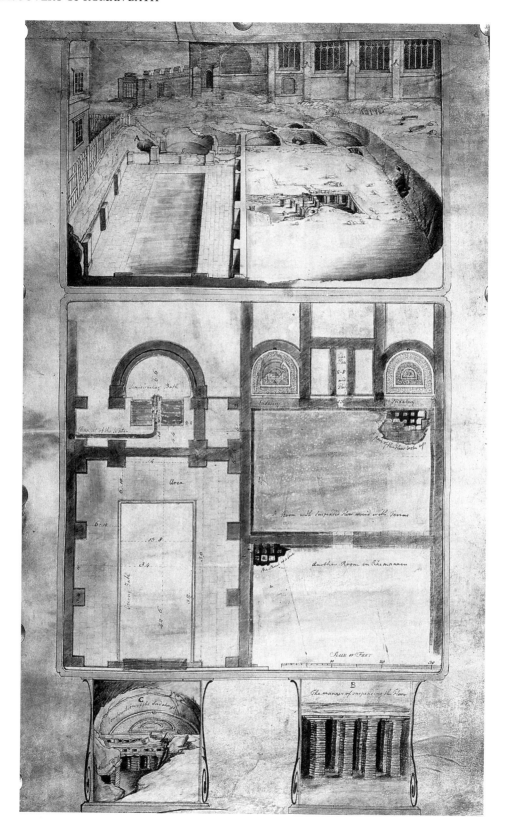

6 *The first major discovery of the baths came in 1755 when the Duke of Kingston's Baths were being constructed. Much of the east end of the Roman bathing establishment was exposed. Fortunately several competent antiquaries were present at the time to record discoveries. The illustration here is of a drawing of 1755 now in the British Museum (No. Add. 21577 Bi).*

7 *During the rebuilding of the Pump Room in 1790 more than seventy sculptured stones were found, many of them belonging to the temple. Although several antiquaries saw them and produced illustrations of varying quality it was not until 1813 that Samuel Lysons published the first accurate account.*

8 *The columns of the temple were of the Corinthian order, with fluted drums and elaborate foliate capitals. The single-surviving capital from the temple was carved in two pieces and shows an unusual leafy tendril growing up on to the abacus. Part of the base of the column has been cut away to allow a low balustrade or railing to butt up to it. The illustration is by Samuel Lysons.*

exposed in 1825, but finds were few and anti-quarian interest waned. A spate of new discoveries, which were to galvanize the archaeo-logical world throughout the rest of the century, began with the arrival in Bath of James Thomas Irvine in 1864 to act as Clerk of Works to Gilbert Scott's restoration of the abbey. Irvine, a meticu-lous man with all the accuracy and skill of a Gothic restorer, immediately fell in love with the city and its past. In his seven years at Bath he amassed volumes of notes on all aspects of the city's history, addressed learned societies and wrote articles for newspapers and national jour-nals. But what is more important, he was an archaeologist of the highest quality, whose ques-tioning mind and accuracy of observation and recording set him well above the vast majority of his contemporaries.

In the year of his arrival, 1864, the old White Hart Inn, on the west side of Stall Street opposite the Pump Room, was derelict. Assessing the 1790 discoveries, Irvine correctly decided that the temple podium probably lay beneath the hotel and obtained leave to excavate in the cellars, appar-ently in the hope of finding a marble floor. No marble floor was discovered, but instead he exposed the solid mass of Roman concrete upon which the temple had stood, the first time that the podium had ever been recorded.

A few years later the superstructure of the inn was demolished and between 1867 and 1869 reconstruction began. Irvine was constantly in the trenches, scribbling measurements on odd mud-spattered scraps of paper and old envelopes, jotting down memos of the principal discoveries in his diaries and in the evenings drawing up fair copies of the records.

Throughout the winter of 1867–8 he was able to record with great accuracy the temple podium (which he had seen three years earlier), a mass of concrete scarred by innumerable pits and distur-bances, from which the facing blocks had been removed at a much earlier date, presumably in the Saxon or medieval period. Around the podium, on the north and west, he recognized the walls of the colonnade surrounding the temple

precinct, and beyond these he noted gravel layers which he considered were probably roads. The work on the foundations of the Grand Pump Room Hotel was completed early in 1868 and by the beginning of the next year the superstructure was almost finished. In March, however, a tunnel was dug beneath Stall Street to join the cellars of the new building with those of the Pump Room. Again Irvine was there finding walls, Roman window-glass and parts of colonnettes and noting them all with his customary diligence. In three years he had seen and recorded most of the tem-ple podium and much of the precinct around it to an accuracy of 6mm (¼in), and in doing so had laid the basis for all future work.

Nor were the Roman Baths to escape his insa-tiable curiosity. In September 1867 he obtained permission to explore the cellars immediately south of the Duke of Kingston's Bath, and in odd moments during the following months he carried out a trial excavation, exposing a semicircular bath, doors and adjacent walls. This was the first purely research excavation to be undertaken in the city. All the time he was keeping watch on the building work on the temple site. In December 1869 the old engine room in the south-west corner of the site was undergoing alterations at the hand of the City Engineer, Major Davis. Irvine, needless to say, was present and busily recorded everything exposed – including a substantial part of a *tepidarium*, a latrine and a number of other details (**9**).

Irvine's reconstruction work on the abbey con-tributed indirectly to the discovery of the sacred spring and reservoir which was to astound the archaeological world in 1879. Earlier, in 1871, he had discovered, apparently by accident, the mas-sive Roman outfall drain, now known to lead excess water from the spring. But after clearing part of it he was forced to abandon the work and shortly afterwards left Bath for another contract.

Fortunately, during his stay in Bath, Irvine had befriended a local builder, Richard Mann, who was later employed by the City Engineer, Major Charles Davis, to carry out much of the initial clearance of the drain and reservoir. Mann wrote regularly to his friend Irvine, describing the

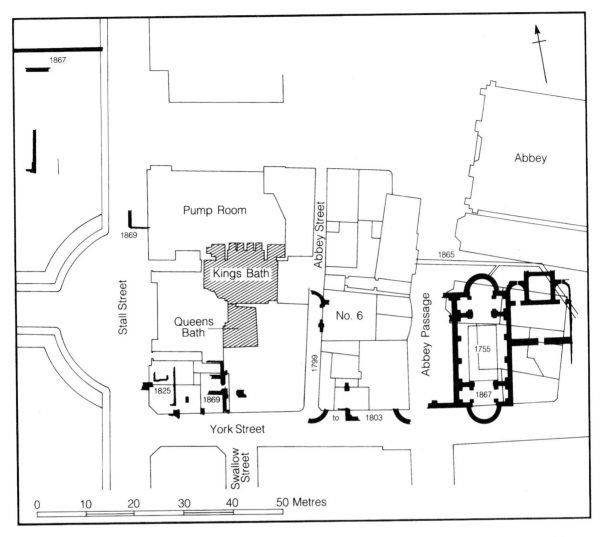

9 *The centre of Bath in 1870 showing the extent of the Roman remains discovered by that date.*

progress of the work and, characteristically, Irvine preserved every letter. These letters are of very considerable importance for the details they provide of the progress of the excavations and of discoveries otherwise unpublished.

Major Davis's involvement with Roman Bath began in earnest in 1871 not long after Irvine had left the city, when, in an attempt to block a leak from the King's Bath, he had his labourers dig a trench along Abbey Passage. About 6m (20ft) down they discovered Roman masonry, now known to be close to the north-west corner of the Great Bath. Using extremely powerful pumps to keep the water-level down, he first explored an area of the ambulatory paving and then exposed the massive steps leading down to the Great Bath.

At the bottom he came upon the sheet lead lining the bath floor and, unable to resist the temptation, cut a 30cm (12in) square out of it to examine the footings beneath. The hole can still be seen when the bath is emptied. At this stage, however, the proprietors of the Kingston Baths began to complain that the pumps had so lowered the water-table that their own bath could no longer be filled. Rather than face legal action, further work was suspended and the trench vaulted over.

Seven years later, in 1878, after the Kingston Baths had been acquired by the city, Davis returned to the problem of the leak. Hoping to improve the drainage he employed Richard Mann to open up the Roman drain from the point where Irvine had found it towards the King's Bath. This meant tunnelling along the line of the largely collapsed drain, barely 1m (3ft 4in) wide, 6m (20ft) below ground – a difficult enough job at any time, but without electric light and in the face of a constant stream of hot mineral water, becoming hotter and more persistent the nearer the tunnellers approached the King's Bath, it must at times have been intolerable. Eventually, within a metre or so of what is now known to be the east wall of the Roman reservoir, it was decided to abandon the westward advance and, raising the level of the tunnel floor to facilitate drainage, to turn north. It was only then that Mann discovered that they were gradually converging on the massive and well-preserved Roman wall running almost parallel to the tunnel on the west side. Excitement mounted as they followed the wall to its north-east corner and then began to tunnel along its north face, finding a well-built door in the centre served by a flight of steps. They were now directly beneath the footings of an eighteenth-century wall of the Pump Room and were digging through mud containing massive blocks of stone from the collapsed Roman buildings.

The work had established beyond doubt that the King's Bath lay within a massive Roman enclosure wall. The next step was inevitable. Davis had the King's Bath drained and soon after the floor was ripped up and the excavation of the Roman reservoir began (**10**). Immediately the excavators came upon a raft of puddled clay which had served as a foundation for the medieval buildings, but once through this they found themselves in a roughly octagonal enclosure, lined with sheets of lead, which surrounded the fissures in the bedrock through which the sacred hot spring issued at the rate of a third of a million gallons a day. Amid the rubble and mud choking the reservoir lay a remarkable array of votive offerings thrown into the waters by the Romans as an act of piety to the goddess Sulis Minerva, or in support of a wish. Fortunately, Major Davis stopped short of digging into these

crucial deposits leaving them intact for us to examine 100 years later.

The discoveries were widely reported in the newspapers and in papers read before learned societies, but before adequate records could be made Davis had the lead stripped from the reservoir and sold 'to furnish sinews for the excavations'. Immediately afterwards the reservoir was floored across with a concrete raft supported on arches, leaving only a small trapdoor to allow a treacherous descent into the almost unbearable atmosphere of the Roman cistern below. Until 1979 this floor served as the base of the King's Bath.

The discoveries of 1878–9 caused a great deal of excitement locally and in an atmosphere of Victorian beneficence a fund was opened, under the sponsorship of the City Council, to buy up the superincumbent properties so that excavation could proceed unhindered. Gradually, throughout 1880–1, those parts of the Great Bath now in public ownership were uncovered, the earth and rubble being removed by a horse and cart trudging up a ramp of earth leading to York Street. No attempt was made to record the stratigraphy. The great vaulted roof which had fallen into the bath was shovelled away without any note being taken, only the larger pieces being left in position, and architectural details were stacked on one side with hardly a mention of their original positions being recorded. Even by the archaeological standards of the time, the activity was little short of disastrous.

But worse was to come as the excavations moved west. The sixteenth-century Queen's Bath was totally destroyed and from 1883 to 1885 the Roman Circular Bath and the adjacent corridors were exposed, and then from 1885 to 1887 the complex of heated baths which constitute the west range was cleared, in what can only be described as a desultory way – immediately to be covered up again by the douche and massage baths, which totally obscured large areas of Roman work before adequate records could be made. There was uproar in the archaeological world. A committee of enquiry, set up by the Society of Antiquaries, was highly critical but had little effect on Davis's activities. He was, after all City Engineer, and his prime responsibility was to provide the city with a new profit-making bathing establishment. The Roman remains were of secondary significance.

The excavations of the mid-1880s were not the end for Davis. In 1890 he was concerned to expose a large room south of the Circular Bath, where a new steam laundry was being constructed. And as late as 1896 a Roman

swimming-bath was uncovered beneath Stall Street at the extreme west end of the establishment. Both features were roofed over but preserved. In sixteen years about two-thirds of the bathing establishment had been uncovered.

Davis continued sporadically to excavate the temple area – particularly between 1893 and 1895, at which time he removed the cellar floors beneath the eighteenth-century Pump Room north of the reservoir and excavated the soil down to the Roman floor levels. This was at the time when the Concert Room was being erected. Very little attention was paid to the remains which, it must be admitted, were unimpressive compared with the great baths exposed a decade before. In the end the cellar floors were replaced on a shuttering, leaving the temple features

10 *The main phase of excavation at the baths took place during the 1880s under the direction of Major Davis. The buildings above were bought up and demolished. The photograph shows the sixteenth-century Queen's Bath in the process of destruction. Beneath it was found the Roman Circular Bath.*

beneath gradually to silt up, totally unrecognized and largely unplanned. Although he did not realize it, he had uncovered much of the temple precinct, part of the sacrificial altar and most of the main entrance to the temple complex.

The half century of discovery ended when, in 1908, Francis Haverfield published the first full account of Roman Bath in *The Victoria County History of Somerset,* preparing the way for a new phase of research.

It is a curious fact that the history of archaeological activity during the twentieth century has been a close reflection of that of the nineteenth century. Very little of any significance happened in the first sixty years with the exception of the re-excavation of the east end of the bathing establishment in 1923 following the demolition of the Duke of Kingston's Bath. It was the creation of the Bath Excavation Committee in 1963, at the instigation of Sir Ian Richmond, that initiated a new era of excavation and research in the city. The committee's brief was to undertake any rescue excavations that were required as a result of development and to design new research programmes to put what was known into a broader context.

The first research programme set up involved the study of the Temple of Sulis Minerva. Trial excavations undertaken in the autumn of 1964 in the cellar beneath the Pump Room established that the Roman structures were well preserved. The next year, 1965, the work was extended by cutting a single trench along a 2.5m (8ft) wide cellar which lay beneath the north part of the Pump Room. Work was difficult and cramped with only 0.6m (2ft) baulks between the trench edge and the cellar walls. The tons of mud and rubble removed were disposed of in adjacent cellars. Everything had to be done beneath the intense heat of glaring arc-lamps, with pumps continually at work to remove surface water. To volunteers accustomed to work in the open air the conditions were at least novel. The rewards, however, were considerable, for not only was the floor of the temple precinct found to be largely intact, but above it lay a mass of collapsed Roman debris including several sculptured blocks, all closely stratified in undisturbed layers of black organic soil which had formed in the late and sub-Roman period.

Among the items recovered was one of the sculptured blocks which had once formed the corner of the Roman sacrificial altar and a dedicatory inscription erected by the augur Lucius Marcius Memor still *in situ* on the precinct floor (**11**). It was an auspicious beginning, but space was severely limited and by 1968 all the exploration that could safely be carried out within the confines of the cellars had been done. The result was that we could at last write a reasonably coherent description of the temple in all its, surprisingly Classical, majesty but there was nothing for the public to see.

In parallel with the work on the temple, a new survey of the Roman Baths was carried out which involved some exploratory excavations in cellars. By Easter 1968 answers had been obtained to most of the major archaeological questions.

By this stage the douche and massage baths, erected by Davis amid such furore in 1886, had become derelict and in 1969 the City Council took the decision to demolish them to make way for a new block of shops and offices. The archaeological problems posed were considerable: not only had Davis used Roman walls as his footings, rendering demolition a highly intricate task, but the new building also required foundations of its own which were an immediate threat to the Roman structures. A satisfactory plan of action was, however, soon agreed. The excavation of 1970–2 enabled the development of the entire west end of the bathing establishment to be studied in full and much of it laid open to view. That so much can now be seen is a tribute to the ingenuity of the architects, but that so much remained to be seen we have to thank Major Davis for his care and concern even in the face of a campaign of vitriolic criticism which we now know to have been largely unfounded.

In 1978 the Bath Archaeological Trust was set up to forward archaeological research in the light of a new and enlightened attitude among local government officials. The first, and most challenging, project undertaken was to excavate that

11 *Trial trench in the cellars beneath the Pump Room, dug in 1965. This exploratory work showed the temple precinct to be extremely well preserved 2m (6½ft) below the cellar floor.*

part of the temple precinct which lay beneath the Pump Room. This entailed a major engineering programme to support the Pump Room floor so that supporting walls could be removed to allow excavators to begin to expose some 3000sq m (3588sq yd) of the Roman buildings which lay 2m (6½ft) beneath the cellar floors.

While plans were in preparation, tragedy struck – a young child died of amoebic meningitis. She had been swimming in the baths and, when the

spring water was tested, it was found to be contaminated. Immediately all the baths (including the Roman Bath) were drained and all supplies of spring water were cut off while experts met to consider the problem. The contamination lay in the almost inaccessible void beneath the King's Bath, which Major Davis had created by roofing the Roman reservoir with a concrete raft. In the autumn of 1979 the reservoir was drained and ventilated so that a detailed exploration could be made.

The results of the survey were quite clear: the nature of the spring was such that there was little chance of ever being able to sterilize the reservoir chamber. The only option was to tap a fresh supply of pure water from well below ground. But the survey had revealed an additional and totally unsuspected problem. The supporting walls which Major Davis had built across the spring, and his underpinning of the south wall of the Pump Room, had subsided to such an extent that major cracks had begun to appear and serious instability had been created. The only solution was to remove the concrete raft and the sagging supports so that the foundations could be consolidated. Now since the foundations were bedded on undisturbed archaeological deposits of the greatest interest, it meant that a rescue excavation had first to be undertaken. Thus it was that in December 1979, after Davis's concrete raft had been taken away, a new programme of archaeological survey and excavation began in the spring almost exactly 100 years after Davis had ceased digging (**12**).

Excavations and trial borings took some while to complete but the results were as spectacular as the work was memorable, providing a rich array of votive offerings as well as fascinating details of the original Roman engineering works. Finally in November 1981, after the underpinning had been completed, a filter bed of sand and gravel was laid in the spring, partly to protect the untouched archaeological deposits and partly to prevent the force of the water from bringing up sand from beneath the footings as had happened for the last century. We had excavated a thickness of about 1.5m (5ft) of silt from half the area

of the reservoir – between a sixth and a quarter of what was there before we began. That so much was left untouched was deliberate policy to ensure that future generations of archaeologists have sufficient of this unique deposit to re-examine when they are ready again to do so.

By Easter 1981 the structural work beneath the Pump Room had been completed and the programme of systematic excavation could at last begin in full sight of a constant flow of visitors.

12 *Excavation in progress in the sacred spring in December 1979. The main spring rises in the centre where the head of the pump stands.*

The intricacy of the excavation and the fact that there were no pressures to finish by a particular time, allowed work to proceed at an unusually gentle pace, until, by January 1983, the last vestiges of soil had been removed and the temple precinct was visible again for the first time in 1500 years.

The excavations of 1978–83 were spectacular. They not only enabled us to understand the temple and baths in a way never before possible, but they allowed the remains to be presented to the public, for the first time, in a coherent and intelligible manner.

The story does not end there. The Bath Archaeological Trust continues to carry out research and rescue excavations in the city and to monitor developments. Major excavations in Swallow Street and Bath Street have added much to our understanding of the core of the Roman settlement, while work to the north, along London Road, shows that dense Roman occupation extended as far as the ancient river crossing near Cleveland Bridge. The discovery of Roman Bath is, and always will be, a continuous process.

3

The temple and its precinct

As the result of the accurate observation and recording undertaken by archaeologists for a quarter of a millennium, the main elements of the temple can now be described (**13**). The temple building itself was arranged astride the main east–west axis of the building complex and placed in the centre of a large colonnaded court-yard, 53 by 74m (174 by 243ft). In front of the temple on the same axis lay the open-air sacrificial altar. The sacred spring and reservoir, the very reason for the existence of Bath, lay in the south-east corner of the temple precinct, immediately south of the altar and so arranged that a north–south visual axis was created from the main hall of the baths to the south, across the spring, to the altar itself. These, then, are the bare

13 *General plan of the temple and spring.*

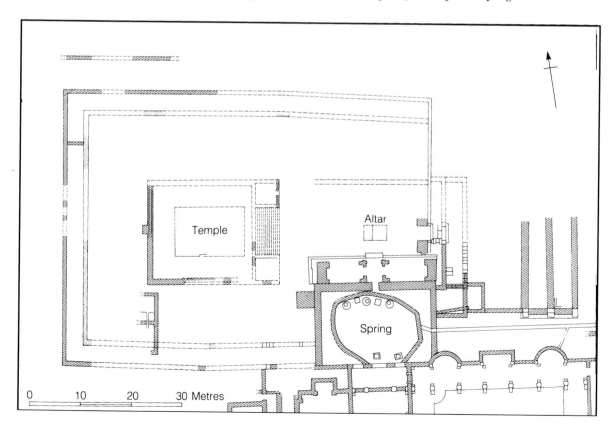

THE TEMPLE AND ITS PRECINCT

bones of the arrangement but, as will become apparent later, the whole conception was richly ornamented with elaborate subsidiary monuments to enliven, improve and excite.

The temple building

Although it is very difficult to get at the temple, most of which lies deep beneath Stall Street, those parts of it that we have been able to examine, together with observations made in the past, show that the building was of two major periods: the original temple put up at the end of the first century AD and an extension added some time later, probably in the second half of the second century or a little later. The original building was constructed on a podium of hard concrete rubble about 9m (29½ft) wide and in the order of 14m (46ft) long, faced with blocks of freestone. Originally the surface of the platform, about 1.5m (5ft) above the surrounding level, would have been reached by a flight of steps built against the east end, but details are at present obscure.

The discoveries of 1790 included six large blocks of stone belonging to the richly decorated triangular pediment which formed the central element of the main front. Just enough of the original survived to allow the entire composition to be pieced together and another block found in 1982 adds further useful details (**14**). It is, without a doubt, one of the most dramatic pieces of sculpture from the whole of Roman Britain (**15, 16, front cover**). In the centre, held aloft by two very Classical-looking winged Victories, is a circular shield bordered by oak wreaths, from the centre of which glowers a Gorgon's head. Although the Gorgon is normally a female in Classical mythology, here in Bath he is shown in the guise of a male with the wedge-shaped nose, the lentoid eyes, moustaches and beetling brow of a Celtic god. His fierce upstanding hair merges into wings and serpents as he stares, in no way incongruously, from his Classical surroundings. The winged Victories perch precariously upon globes, while beyond them, in the corners of the pediment, are figures thought possibly to be tritons, but too little of them now survives to be

sure. Below the shield, filling the spaces between its curved lower edge and the drapery of the Victories, are two helmets, one in the form of a dolphin's head, the other providing a perch for a rather startled owl, rooted to the ground by two hands clasping his wings. Both owl and dolphin are attributes closely linked to Minerva.

It is difficult to escape from the view that the Bath Gorgon is a visual conflation of the Classical Gorgon and a manifestation of the Celtic god or goddess Sulis, who is presented here perhaps in the guise of a sun god. The purely Classical surroundings and the attributes of Minerva are, however, a strong reminder of the Roman take-over. The pediment is truly a brilliant merging of the two traditions and provides a fitting centre-piece for the temple dedicated to Sulis Minerva.

If the survival of a large part of the pediment was fortunate, so too was the discovery in 1790 of a number of blocks belonging to the cornice which surrounded it (**17**). All the sections now remaining are richly decorated with a continuous band of flowers, leaves, tendrils and bunches of fruit, reminiscent in some degree of work found in northern and eastern Gaul. Whether or not the Bath cornice was carved by a Gaulish craftsman must remain an open question while so little is known of the origin and development of local British schools of sculpture, but the similarities between the Bath and Gaulish work are certainly suggestive of close contact. Interesting proof that the cornice did in fact belong to the Gorgon's head pediment was provided by one of the blocks from the raking cornice, that is the cornice lying above one of the sloping upper edges of the pediment. The lower edge of this particular block had been cut at an angle to join the surface of the horizontal cornice along the bottom of the pediment; the angle matched that of the lower corner of the pediment.

Below the pediment would have been a frieze and architrave supported by the columns of the temple front. The frieze is completely unknown, but in such surroundings it must have been elaborately decorated. There is very little of the

14 *Reconstruction of the temple front. Compare with Lysons's drawing (7).*

0   5   10   15   20   25 Feet

0   1   2   3   4   5   6   7   8 Metres

15 *Parts of the temple pediment and its cornice, found in 1790 when the Pump Room was built, have been reassembled in the Roman Baths Museum.*

16 *The centre-piece of the temple pediment. It shows a male version of a Gorgon's head – a superb example of the conflation of Roman and Celtic art styles.*

architrave, except for one small fragment, again found in 1790, inscribed with the well-cut letters VM, 11cm (4½in) high (**18**). It is very tempting to see this as the end of the word TEMPLUM, but unfortunately unless more of it is found the matter will remain unresolved.

The columns of the main temple front are known from pieces discovered in 1790, in the spring in 1879 and again in the temple precinct in 1982 (**19, 20**). The massive, simple Attic bases (1.14m (3ft 9in) in diameter), fluted shafts and elaborately carved Corinthian capitals, rising to a height of about 8m (26ft), are grandiose monumental architecture of a kind very rare in Britain.

Again, stylistic considerations suggest the hand of an eastern Gaulish master craftsman. Knowing the proportions of the columns there can be little doubt that the temple was tetrastyle, that is, there were four columns supporting the pediment. This fact, taken together with the width of the pediment, suggests that the whole

33

17 *One of the highly decorated cornice blocks from the main temple front.*

front would have been about 9m (30ft) wide which exactly fits the estimated width of the podium.

The columns preserved from 1790 were all hollowed out from behind leaving a skin barely 15cm (6in) thick. This was thought to imply that the surviving fragments were from half or three-quarter columns set back against the wall of the cella, rather than from the main columns of the temple front. However, it is now clear that most of the sculptured fragments found in 1790, including the Gorgon's head pediment, were thinned down soon after discovery by sawing off the backs. This kind of treatment was quite normal in the eighteenth century and we may reasonably suppose that the hollowing of the columns took place at the same time. That all the

18 *The inscribed fragment of the architrave.*

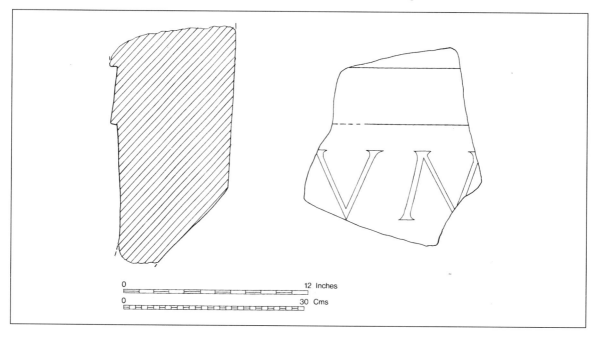

| 0 | | | | | | | | 12 Inches |
| 0 | | | | | | | | 30 Cms |

fragments found in 1879 and 1982 were of solid columns adds support to this view. This means that there is no longer any reason to argue for a pseudoperipteral arrangement (i.e. half columns set against a cella).

How, then, were the different elements of the original temple laid out? The simplest explanation would be to suppose that the plan was prostyle, that is, the four-column front was separated from a simple cella by a short porch (or pronaos). Such

19 *The capital of one of the four columns of the temple front found in 1790.*

20 *Reconstruction of the entablature of the temple.*

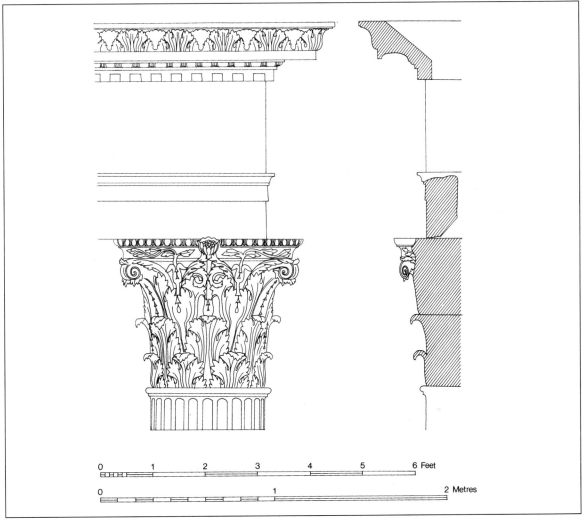

0   1   2   3   4   5   6 Feet

0   1   2 Metres

an arrangement would fit quite well with the proportions of the podium. Whether the actual plan was like this, or one of the more complex variants, we are unlikely to know until the entire podium has been excavated, and even then the crucial evidence may well have been destroyed.

The early temple was doubled in size, probably in the late second century. This seems to have been done by leaving the original structure intact and enclosing it within a surrounding ambulatory incorporating a monumental east front. How the ambulatory was treated we cannot say: it may have been little more than a raised walkway around the original building but the revetting wall could have supported columns and there may even have been a lean-to roof resting against the temple sides. The new front was an ingenious construction designed so as to leave the original façade entirely visible when viewed from the east. Immediately in front of it was a new flight of

21 *The steps of the temple exposed in 1981 immediately against the west wall of the Pump Room. The steps were very worn and had been partly cut back so that new treads could be added.*

stone stairs flanked on either side by small rooms, very probably subsidiary shrines. The middle part of the flight of steps was exposed in 1981 just outside the west wall of the Pump Room. The steps showed very considerable wear and had been cut back to take new treads, fragments of which still survived (**21**). An even earlier flight of steps could be seen in places beneath. That limestone steps could wear to this extent is a reflection of both the popularity of the building and the hobnail boots and sandals of the Romano-British population!

Of the flanking shrines very little is known, because the west wall of the Pump Room has obscured so much, but the position of the front of the north shrine has been located. The step upon which the superstructure was built was carefully examined and from the wear marks and discolorations due to weathering, still traceable on it, it was possible to show that the wall had been enlivened by corner pilasters and that the room was entered through a central door.

The rebuilding would have turned what was a purely Classical temple into one far more like the native Romano-Celtic temples found all over north-western Europe. It is yet another fascinating example of the mixing of Classical and native ideas, on what was after all the extreme fringe of the Roman empire. The Classical temple, put up, no doubt, under official patronage in the first century, was modified to suit local tastes and rituals a generation or two later by which time the local population had gained a new assurance under Roman rule and Romano-British architecture had come of age.

The sacrificial altar

About 15m (49ft) in front of the temple stood the great sacrificial altar, at the point where the two principal visual axes of the temple complex crossed. All that survived in position was the raised platform of limestone slabs, still clamped together with ties of iron, upon which the altar had stood. The main platform measured 2.8m (9ft) square and by tracing the worn and weathered areas around the edge, it was possible to show that the superstructure of the altar must have been 2.4m (8ft) square.

By a remarkable series of chances we are able to reconstruct the altar in some detail. The first indication of what it would have looked like came in 1965 when, in a trial trench dug across the altar platform, one of the decorated altar corners was found, carved on two adjacent faces with deities (**22**). One of the deities depicted is a naked male, probably Bacchus. His companion, on the adjacent side, is a heavily draped female holding an upturned vase, from which liquid flows, merging with her drapery. In the crook of her right arm she supports what appears to be a cornucopia.

Within a few minutes of making the discovery a quick inspection of the museum showed that a closely similar block had been found during the rebuilding of 1790 (**23**). Although badly weathered, it is possible to recognize the same paired deities, one naked, the other clothed. In this case the naked god was Hercules Bibax, shown holding a large drinking vessel in one hand, the other resting on a knobbed club. Over his shoulders he wears a cape made of a lion's skin. The adjacent figure is Jupiter, holding a trident in one hand while at his feet stands an eagle. Exactly where the stone was found is not recorded but, since the north wall of the 1790 Pump Room actually crosses the altar, it is not at all impossible that it was found there, within a metre or two of the 1965 discovery.

By an even more remarkable coincidence a third corner is known, built into the corner buttress of the church at Compton Dando, 13km (8 miles) west of Bath. The block, now exposed to all weathers, is very badly eroded, but here again two adjacent figures can be traced, one naked, the other clothed. Unfortunately the naked figure is too weathered to allow identification, but his (or her) partner is shown with one foot on a rock, raised knee supporting a musical instrument and is therefore either Apollo or Orpheus. There can be very little doubt that all three blocks belong to the same monument: they are identical in size and base mouldings, and the pairing of the deities, one clothed, the other naked, is consistent. Moreover, stylistic similarities such as the body stance and the exceptionally thick necks provide a strong indication that all three were carved at least by the same school, if not by the same craftsman. How and why the Compton Dando block was dragged 13km from Bath we are unlikely to know, but it might be significant that both Compton Dando church and the central area of Bath, beneath which the altar lies, belonged to the same religious establishment. Perhaps cart-loads of old building stone, including the altar corner, were removed from the centre of Bath in the Middle Ages and used in adjacent church buildings. This is pure guesswork but it is at least possible.

We have, then, three of the four corner blocks of the altar, each with integral base mouldings but without the necessary capping mould. Fortunately, during the 1965 excavation, one of the moulded blocks which would have formed the working surface of the altar was discovered lying amid the rubble, close to the corner stone. Its cornice mouldings were simply carved in a style admirably suited to match the base, while its upper surface, which would have been exposed, was very carefully tooled to a smooth finish and slightly dished: this would have been a very distinct advantage during sacrifices, particularly when freshly slaughtered animals were being opened up for purposes of augury (**24, 25**).

The 1965 trench, immediately in front of the altar, produced another remarkable discovery. Standing on the flagged floor of the temple precinct was a statue base (see **11**) inscribed DEAE SVLI (To the Goddess Sulis) L.MAR-CIVS MEMOR (Lucius Marcius Memor) HARVSP (Haruspex) D.D. (gave this gift). A *haruspex* was a high-ranking augur whose job it was to foretell the future by examining the entrails of sacrifices made on the altar, or by interpreting the flight patterns of birds and other omens. It is interesting to know that the temple at Bath was of sufficient importance to attract a man of this status, who might normally be expected to practise only in the largest centres of the empire. It will be seen from the illustration (**26**) that Memor's title had at first been abbreviated HAR, regularly laid

22 *The altar corner discovered in 1965 was carved on two adjacent sides with deities, one male, the other female. The naked male is the god Bacchus who holds a thyrsus and pours a drink to a panther squatting at his feet. The goddess cannot easily be identified, but the cornucopia which she holds beneath one arm and the libation flowing from the upturned vessel suggest that she is connected with fertility. Approx. 1.26m (4ft) high.*

out in relation to the other lettering, and only later was the VSP jammed in rather awkwardly at the end. It may be that *haruspices* were so rare in Britain that no one in Bath knew what HAR stood for and the temple authorities had to be more explicit.

The base had been placed on the latest paving level a little to the west of the altar: it is therefore not part of the original layout, but was probably added late in the temple's life. The gift which Memor dedicated to the goddess was in all probability a statue erected immediately to the east of the

23 *Altar corner discovered in 1790. The clothed male figure is Jupiter, the naked male is the drinking Hercules – Hercules Bibax – who wears a lion-skin cloak, the paws knotted across his chest, and rests his left hand on a knobbed club. Approx. 1.26m (4ft) high.*

inscription. Sadly nothing now survives of it except for a slot cut in the paving stones to take its base.

Again then, by a fortunate combination of chance discovery and planned excavation, it has been possible to reconstruct, almost in its entirety, another of the town's major religious monuments. The great sacrificial altar emerges as a 1.5m (5ft) high mass of stone, with elaborately carved corners set on a raised platform in such a position that it would form the visual focus from all around. Memor's gift would have enhanced its dignity even more.

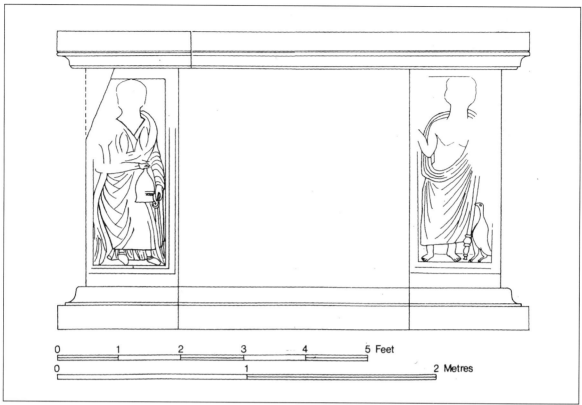

24 *The altar reconstructed.*

25 *The altar corners replaced on their original base in the temple precinct.*

26 *The trial excavation of 1965 exposed a dedicatory inscription still in its original position on the precinct floor. It records a gift, probably a statue, erected for the goddess Sulis Minerva by the temple augur* (haruspex) *Lucius Marcius Memor.*

The enclosing colonnade

The temple, altar and the spring (to be described below) were enclosed in a single unified concept by a colonnaded veranda running along the north, west and south sides of the precinct. The east side was closed by a blank wall through which opened the main entrance. Most of the colonnade is now below parts of the town which cannot be excavated, but substantial sections of the north and west sides were seen by Irvine in 1867 and again by Wedlake in 1960 while the west side was once more exposed before destruction in 1986. Part of the south side lay beneath the cellars of Stall Street, and in 1964 and 1968 trenches were dug to examine, at first hand, the details of its structure. As a result we now know that the outer wall was a blank enclosing wall serving to seal off the temple from the outside world, but 3m (10ft) inside it was a ground-level stylobate (a foundation of large flat stone blocks), originally fronted by a stone gutter the position of which could still be traced. The stylobate would once have supported a colonnade which, in turn, would have taken a veranda roof sloping inwards so that the rain-water would drain into the gutter. The overall result would have been to create a cloistered feeling, the veranda providing protection from rain and shade from the sun.

The temple occupied much of the western part of the precinct. Around it the precinct floor was simply gravel. The eastern part was differently treated. Strictly it was divided into three: a central paved area around the altar (the inner precinct) (**colour plate 2**), a southern part wholly occupied by the sacred spring, and a northern area about which little is known but which appears to have been simply surfaced with gravel. The paved area and the spring have been examined in considerable detail in the excavation programme of 1979 to 1983 and the entire structural history can now be worked out in fascinating detail.

The sacred spring and the inner precinct

The reason for the siting of the temple and the baths was the great spring which gushed out a third of a million gallons of mineral waters a day at a temperature of 42°C. Endowed, no doubt, with religious and curative properties by the pre-Roman inhabitants, it is not surprising that the Romans should have been so quick to exploit it (**colour plates 3, 4**).

The great volume of water must have created very serious difficulties for the Roman engineers and until the problems of its control were solved the central complex of public buildings could not be built. The first stage in the process of taming the waters would have been the creation of an efficient drainage system to remove excess water while building was in progress. Most of the great drain built at this time can still be followed and indeed it has been restored to its original Roman function of carrying off waste. It was built of rough stone walling of such proportions that a man could comfortably walk along it without stooping. In the bottom was a rectangular timber-lined gully to take the flow, with the timbers still preserved. At intervals along its length smaller

subsidiary drains emptied in. Realizing that at such points and at changes in alignment there was the possibility of silting or of the clogging of inlets, the careful Roman engineers constructed rectangular manholes leading up to the street surface to provide those responsible for keeping the drains in good order with easy access. Once clear of the central area of the settlement, the drain appears to have emptied into an open leat which must originally have led to the River Avon. Now, however, the Roman drain flows into a complex network of medieval and later sewers before reaching the river.

As soon as the drain was in operation work could begin on the creation of a reservoir. The drain had conveniently lowered the water-level at the spring head, enabling the engineers to get close to the vent. Next a ring-beam of close-spaced oak piles was rammed into the mud in a rough circle around all the outlets leaving a gap at the mouth of the drain. The piles served to consolidate the ground and provided a convenient

working surface from which the mud and silt in the spring could be dug out. This done a foundation trench was then dug around the outside of the ring of piles and its bottom consolidated with piles to form a firm bedding for the reservoir wall. The wall was built of massive stone blocks, tightly fitted together without mortar, and rose to a maximum height of 2m (6½ft) above the inner pile ring. In its base, at the east side, a 30cm (1ft) square vent was left for the water to escape into the drain and above the vent a sluice slot was created. Some idea of how the work may have appeared at this stage is given by **27**.

When the wall was complete the important process of water proofing began. First, blue lias clay was puddled in around the tops of the

27 *Diagram showing an early stage in the construction of the reservoir. Excess water is carried away in the drain. The ring of piles consolidates the mud providing a convenient working platform. The reservoir wall of massive stone blocks is shown beginning to rise.*

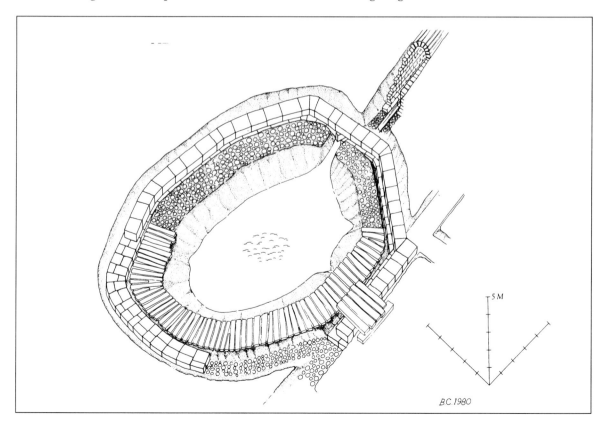

B.C. 1980

5 M

wooden piles. Then the entire reservoir wall was lined inside with massive sheets of lead 1cm (*c.* ½in) thick, measuring some 2.4 by 1.8m (8 by 6ft) and each weighing nearly half a ton. The upper edges were folded back across the wall while the lower edge was bent out and the lower angle sealed with a thick step of waterproof pink concrete with tiles set into the top. The vertical joins were made good by overlapping the sheets and burning the edges together (**28, 29**). The overall effect was to create a massive lead-lined container into which the water gushed through natural fissures in the base.

How the sluice slot was treated we do not know but it could simply and effectively have been sealed with baulks of timber. All this time the bottom vent was allowing the water to flow away. Finally, when the plumbing was complete, the vent was blocked with 30cm (1ft)-square timber (which remained in position until Major Davis removed it in 1878!). Immediately the water would have risen until the reservoir was full and it was from the top that the hot water was channelled off to fill the Great Bath. At first sight it might seem rather unnecessary to go to such lengths simply to provide a constant flow for the bath, but the Roman engineers understood the waters well. They knew that the rapid flow brought up quantities of sand which would have clogged the plumbing in no time. By building the reservoir with its 2m (6½ft) head of water they ensured that the sediment would settle so that the water flowing from the top into the bath was clear. The sediment would, of course, have accumulated in the reservoir but it could be flushed out quite easily by opening the sluice, from time to time, allowing the head of water to wash the silt away through the main drain. It must have been with this problem in mind that the drain was constructed on a grand scale. Standing back from all the detail, there is no doubt that the engineers were highly skilled and were fully aware of the potential, and the difficulties, of the source. Their solution to the problem was as elegant as it was efficient.

We have been concerned so far with technical questions but we must not forget the context.

The spring was a sacred location and was enclosed within the temple precinct. It therefore had to be visually emotive as befits a place where the underworld of the gods was in communication with the everyday world. The simple elegance of the reservoir, full of hot bubbling water, deep green with a pall of vapour floating above the surface, cannot have failed to have impressed.

In the early stages the spring was open to the air, surrounded only by a low balustrade. On the south side was the hall of the bathing establishment penetrated by three large openings so that visitors could see the spring and come close to the sacred water, in exactly the same way as tourists do today (**30**). To the north the entire area in front of the temple was paved on one level with massive slabs of limestone and in the centre was the altar. The eastern boundary at this stage was a plain wall perforated only by the main precinct entrance immediately opposite the altar. The emphasis of the entire layout was on simple uncluttered elegance.

The reservoir enclosure

Towards the end of the second century a dramatic, and indeed monumental, change was made to the temple precinct – the reservoir was enclosed within a massive rectangular chamber roofed with a tile and concrete vault. The thick walls of the enclosure, built of regular ashlar masonry with tile courses at intervals, still stand to a height of between 1 and 2m (3–6½ft) and can be seen along the north and east sides. The only means of access was a single narrow door set in the centre of the north wall directly south of the altar, presumably the way by which the officiating priest approached the spring. As part of this programme of renovation the height of the reservoir wall had been raised by about a metre. This meant that to give easy access from the precinct level three steps had to be provided up to the door-sill, which was at the new level of the reservoir top.

Where the east wall crossed the outfall an arch was created above the capstone which covered

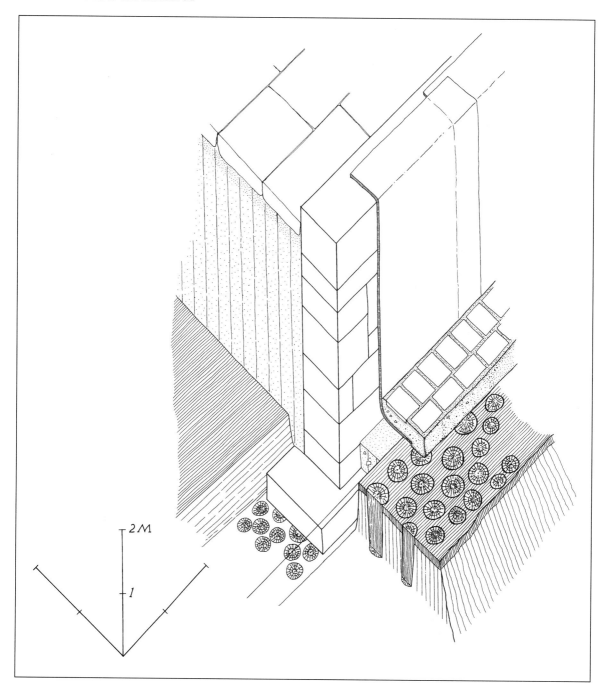

28 *Diagrammatic section through the reservoir wall and its foundations showing the way in which the waterproof lining of lead sheets was arranged.*

the drain. In recent times water has been allowed to gush through the arch creating an impressive cascade, but it is difficult to see how this could have happened in the original arrangement since the Roman sluice slots are at too low a level. Moreover the courses of ashlar immediately above the capstone appear once to have continued across. The simplest explanation is that the arch was a relieving arch designed to take the weight of the wall off the capstone and that it was originally

infilled with ashlar work. Massive steps down to the drain at this point have in the past been referred to as leading to a 'dipping place' where the water could be drunk. A more mundane (and more likely) suggestion is that they simply provided access to the drainage system to enable the sluice to be opened from time to time.

29 *The reservoir during excavation. The wall blocks can be seen (left) stripped of their lead by Major Davis. The oak piles are still very well preserved. The massive pier was probably the base for a statue standing at what would have been the Roman water-level.*

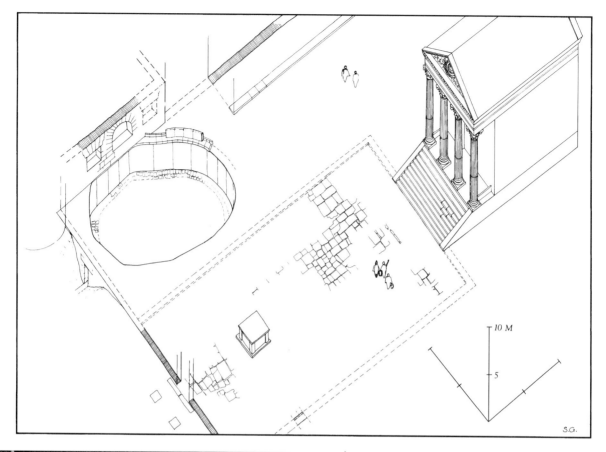

S.G.

30 *The temple precinct in the late first century AD.*

31 *The vault which once roofed the reservoir enclosure collapsed and fell into the spring. The spine of the vault and its brick ribs can clearly be seen (cf. 32).*

We have said that the reservoir enclosure was roofed. Dramatic evidence for this came from the excavation of the spring into which the great vault had collapsed (**31**). The excavation revealed most of its structural details – a spine of voussoir stones with brick ribs at intervals, the spaces between the ribs being filled with hollow box-tiles to relieve the weight. So complete was the surviving detail that we can confidently offer a reconstruction (**32**). The only point of uncertainty is the nature of the openings in the lunettes: they must have existed to allow the steam to escape but no evidence of the detailed arrangement survives. Nor are we certain how the vault was finished but it was certainly coated with a layer of waterproof pink mortar and in all

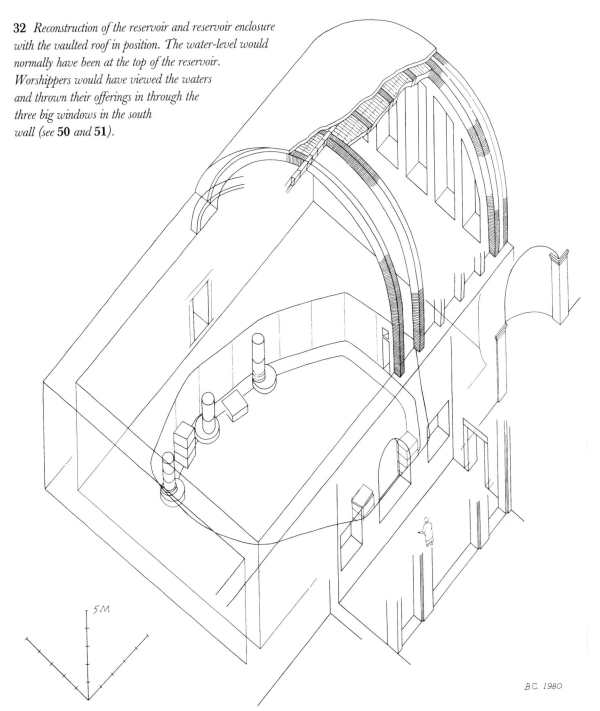

32 *Reconstruction of the reservoir and reservoir enclosure with the vaulted roof in position. The water-level would normally have been at the top of the reservoir. Worshippers would have viewed the waters and thrown their offerings in through the three big windows in the south wall (see 50 and 51).*

5M

B.C. 1980

probability was left as a stark, unadorned concrete vault – a monument to technical competence: the Romans were never too worried about exteriors.

Interiors were another matter. The reservoir enclosure captured the spring in a watery gloom. Luxuriant ferns and mosses sprouting from the walls, birds swooping in and out, and the constant bubbling of the waters, would together have created the atmosphere of a vast natural grotto. It is difficult to believe that the enclosure was built for any reason other than to enhance the air of mystery, to impress the worshipper with the sanctity of the place. The effect was highlighted in another way. Seven massive bases were built up from the reservoir bottom to the surface of the water. Three were circular and four were square: all were only roughly dressed but since they would have been entirely beneath the water this would not have mattered. Of their purpose we can only speculate, the most satisfying suggestion being that the bases supported statues – perhaps of water nymphs and gods – or a combination of statues and columns. On a cold winter morning, when white steam was swirling above the water, the effect of the floating figures in the limpid half-light would have been electrifying.

At a more practical level, the construction of the reservoir necessitated other changes. Since a considerable volume of water would pour off the vault into the precinct, a ground-level gutter had to be set in the paving outside the north wall of the reservoir to drain water away to the main outfall. There were also some changes made to the eastern boundary wall involving a considerable thickening particularly of the gate which may have been monumentalized at this stage. Finally, it was quite probably at this period that the temple was extended in the manner described above. Together these rebuildings would have changed the original temple complex out of all recognition.

The inner precinct in the third and fourth centuries

The great reservoir enclosure was a construction of no small technical skill. The flanks of the vault must have exerted a considerable thrust on the north and south walls but this was anticipated. The south wall already existed: it was thin but the buttressing effect of the side walls of the hall to the south meant that no additional thickening was needed. The new north wall, however, was built twice the thickness and no doubt had massive foundations in addition. Even so this was not enough.

Gradual subsidence or settling must have occurred. There would probably have been signs of cracking and then the north-east corner seems to have sheared away. Immediate remedial action had to be taken, but the problem was how to provide strengthening buttressing along the north wall without making the structure unsightly and impinge too much upon the precinct.

The solution adopted was both inspired and effective. Quite simply a raised portico was created

33 *The temple precinct after excavation looking east across the altar towards the entrance. The raised portico (right) was built in front of the reservoir enclosure, part of the wall of which can be seen with its small central door leading to the spring.*

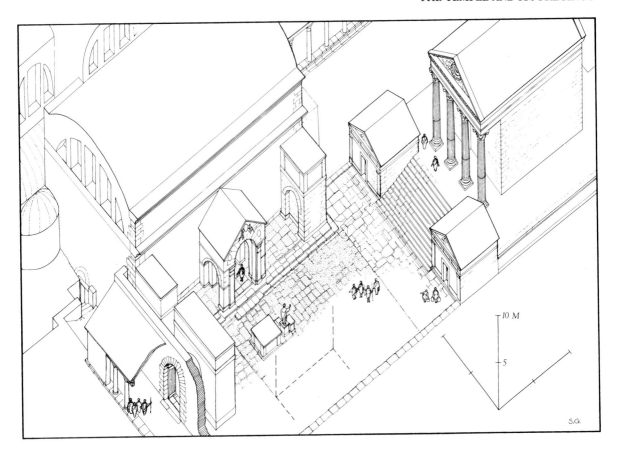

34 *The temple precinct in the late third century AD.*

along the entire north wall incorporating three buttresses (**33**). At both the north-east and north-west corners these buttresses were massively built of large stone blocks clamped together with iron ties. The north-west buttress seems to have been in the form of an arch, but since it was taken down and replaced later the details are obscure. The north-east buttress was quite solid but with a recess in the west face echoing the width of the western arch. The central buttress was disguised as a quadrifrons (a two-way arch with four supports), the whole serving as a monumental porch to the door leading to the spring. How the rest of the structure was treated is less clear though there were probably additional piers along the new façade supporting an entablature, and quite possibly the portico behind was vaulted (**34**). The overall effect of these additions was to create a solid buttressing mass along the entire length of the north wall giving the appearance of a grandiose façade.

The centre-piece of this new arrangement was the monumental porch (**35**) of which the lower parts of the front piers remain in position and blocks of the upper part have been found lying in the rubble collapse. From these it is possible to give some idea of the superstructure. It seems that the main doorway was an arched opening flanked by pilasters which would have supported an entablature. Unusually for north-western Europe, the arch was set in a triangular pediment which was elaborately sculpted. Although only a few of the original blocks survive they are sufficient to show the general arrangement – a central rock from which water is gushing – flanked by two lightly clothed water nymphs (**36**) holding a roundel above the rock, in which was probably depicted the head of the god Sol – the god of the sun. The symbolism is quite clear – Sol presiding over the waters – a highly appropriate design for

35 *Reconstruction of the façade of the quadrifrons.*

such a position, only a few metres from the narrow door giving access to the spring! It raises the very interesting question of whether Sulis was also a sun god in Celtic mythology. If so the conflation of the male Sulis with the female Minerva would be most unusual but in the Celtic fringes this amusing play of opposites may well have been acceptable – it was very much in the Celtic spirit and we shall meet it again in a moment.

Now, it will be evident that the new portico impinged quite considerably upon the inner precinct and would have created an unacceptable asymmetry, unless, that is, an equivalent façade of some kind was erected to the north of the altar to maintain a visual balance. Unfortunately, this area is now entirely obscured by the north wall of the Pump Room and we will never know for certain what was done, but from the mass of tumbled stone recovered in the general area at various times during the last 300 years comes part of a monumental façade known as the Façade of the Four Seasons (for details see below, pp.55–8) which may well have occupied this position. The idea is even more attractive when we note that the Façade probably incorporated a pediment with the head of the moon goddess, Luna, in the centre (see **41–3**). It would have been a most satisfying balance to have had the moon goddess, Luna, facing the sun god, Sol, across the altar: again the tension of paired opposites!

The buttressing of the reservoir wall necessitated the removal of part of the eastern wall of the precinct which was rebuilt further to the east with a colonnaded walk on the outside. The original monumental eastern door was retained and was joined to the new doorway by a stylobate which may well have taken a screen wall of some kind to obscure a rather unsightly backwater in

36 One of the blocks of the pediment of the quadrifrons depicting part of a nymph.

the south-eastern corner of the reconstructed precinct. The retention of the old doorway is interesting: it was structurally unnecessary, and indeed inconvenient, but since it marked the original entrance to the precinct it must have had symbolic significance as a boundary marker and thus had to be kept even though it would have been far simpler to have demolished it altogether.

The construction of the portico marked a major stage in the history of the temple and saw the monument at its most elaborate. Thereafter what changes there were were comparatively minor.

It seems that there were still problems with the stability of the north-west corner of the reservoir enclosure. Eventually the arched buttress was pulled down and a new solid buttress, echoing that at the east end of the portico, was put up together with a new buttress against the west wall. The alterations disturbed the regularity of the portico façade, all of which, except for the quadrifrons, was pulled down. It was as part of this programme of alterations that the steps of the portico were renewed and the portico, together with the area around the altar, was repaved with slabs of blue pennant sandstone. Later alterations were much less significant and gradually the old precinct began to take on a shabby, patched appearance, before decay finally set in.

The spring and the worshippers

The spring held a considerable power over visitors to the temple because it was here that they could come closest to the divinities of the underworld and in particular to Sulis Minerva who presided over the waters. The simplest way to communicate with the goddess was to throw messages and offerings into the water, and this was done with great enthusiasm throughout the 400 years of the temple's life. Heavy objects thrown in would sink to the bottom of the reservoir and into the quicksand below, where the constant turbulence of the spring would churn them up all together. Lighter objects would float or lie in the surface of the sand only to be washed into the drain when the sluice was opened. When Richard Mann opened up the drain in 1878 many valuable

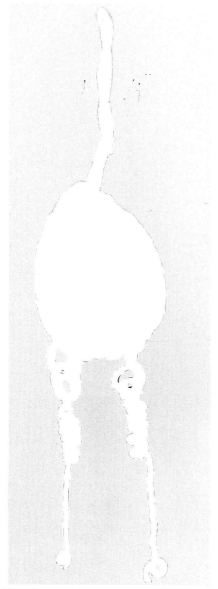

37 Gold earring with inset carbuncle from the spring. Overall length 3.7cm (1½in).

38 Larger than life-size mask of tin which had once been attached to a wooden backing. The wood prevented the mask from sinking to the bottom of the reservoir and caused it to float out into the culvert where it was found 1,500 years later. Presumably it would originally have served in one of the temple rituals. Height 33cm (13in).

items were found. A gold earring with an inset carbuncle (**37**), a pin with a pearl attached, and a bag containing 33 exquisitely engraved gemstones (**colour plate 5**) – all were presumably thrown into the spring and were washed into the culvert. One of the most dramatic objects to be found at this time was a ceremonial tin mask (**38**), quite probably a ritual object belonging to the temple.

The heavier objects sank into the silts of the spring and there remained, the collapsed vaulted roof eventually sealing them in. When Major Davis cleared the spring he left most of the fallen vault in position, but around the edges, where the silt was higher, resting on the tile surround, he was able to excavate part of the ritual deposit producing large numbers of coins, several pewter vessels and a curse inscribed on a sheet of pewter. This was a foretaste of things to come for in 1979 and 1980 we were able to remove the collapsed vault and dig deeper into the ritual deposit filling the spring.

What emerged was a remarkable display of offerings (**colour plate 6**): 10–20,000 coins, many silver and four gold; handled cups and other metal vessels of pewter, silver and bronze inscribed with dedications to the goddess Sulis Minerva; a large collection of some 90 pewter curses; a magnificent inlaid penannular brooch (**colour plate 7**) and a range of other items

39 *Ivory votive offering, probably symbolic of female breasts. From the spring. 7cm (2¾in) across.*

including the head of a ritual silver rattle, floral bronze decorations possibly from the priests' robes, an amulet of breasts carved from elephant ivory (**39**) and, rather incongruously, a bronze washer from a model of a ballista (a kind of large-scale spring gun).

The vast quantity of coinage gives some idea of how powerful the goddess was in the minds of the worshippers. Although much of it was low-value bronze and brass there was a number of silver denarii, worth a day's pay for a working man, and four gold coins each of which would have meant two months' salary for a fairly high-ranking official – altogether a rather different level of response from the 2p and 10p pieces which today's visitors throw into the circular bath!

The metal vessels, jugs, handled cups, plates and bowls are particularly interesting (**40**). Many of them are inscribed to the goddess and it is quite possible that at least some of the pieces were the temple plate, discarded in this way when worn out or replaced. The prevalence of handled cups raises the question of whether the waters were drunk, but this seems unlikely and in all probability the vessels were used for pouring libations.

But it is the curses that bring us closest to the people. To inspire the goddess to work on your

40 *Two pewter and one silver paterae found together with others in the sacred spring in 1979–80. All were inscribed with dedications to the goddess Sulis Minerva.*

behalf it would have been necessary to write a message, in correct official language, on a sheet of pewter and to consign it to the waters, either flat (**colour plate 8**) or rolled up. A typical curse would ask the goddess to bring down some terrible vengeance on someone who had done you wrong and there would follow a list of suspects among whom the goddess would know which one to punish. The curse found by Major Davis is a good example of this; it begins: 'May he who carried off Vilbia from me become as liquid as the water. May she who so obscenely devoured her become dumb', and then follows a list of eight suspects. This, at any rate, was the traditional reading but there is now some doubt as to its accuracy and the suggestion has been made that what was carried off was not a girl but a bath towel, rather spoiling the possibilities of turning the curse into a good story!

Another of the same kind found in 1979 reads: 'To the Goddess Sulis Minerva [from] Docca. I give to your divinity the money which I have lost [by theft], that is five denarii; and may he who [has stolen it] whether slave [or free, whether man or woman] is to be compelled...' and here the curse breaks off. Another is even more interesting: 'Whether pagan or Christian, whosoever, whether man or woman, whether boy or girl, whether slave or free, has stolen from me, Annianus, in the morning six silver pieces from my purse, you, lady Goddess, are to extract [them] from him. If through some deceit he has given me [...], and do not give thus to him, but [...] his blood who has invoked this on me.' The second side of the sheet lists eighteen suspects. Here, the aggrieved Annianus is hedging his bets in all directions. The first part is all-embracing enough to make sure no one was excluded. The second part, though rather obscure, seems to be an attempt to make any counter spell which the thief had set in motion rebound on him. The inclusion of the word 'Christian' clearly implies that in the fourth century Christianity had firmly established itself even in such an ancient pagan town as Bath.

It is tempting to wonder whether Annianus was not also responsible for a second curse which simply reads: 'I have given to the goddess, Sulis, the six silver pieces which I have lost. It is for the goddess to extract it from the debtors written below.' Three names are listed among whom one, Senicianus, also occurs on the first curse. Could it be that having failed with this one, Annianus had another written with a longer list of suspects and more all-embracing wording? While it is possible, the recurrence of the name and the similarity of the sum may be nothing more than coincidence.

It is clear from two of those quoted that a kind of official language was being used 'whether it be X or Y', rather like the all-inclusive language of solicitors today. Without the correct wording a curse would fail or misfire. No doubt one had to pay (then as now) to have an expert write the draft. In this respect it is particularly interesting that the last curse mentioned ended with the statement, 'The draft has been copied.' What exactly this means is not clear but it could be that the scribe wrote a draft which the person placing the curse then copied out on a pewter sheet with his own hand. This could explain the variety of handwritings.

So far we have considered only the curses dealing with people who stole things. Money, a bath towel, a bracelet and a hooded cloak are all mentioned – but another use of the divine power was adjudicating in disputes. This is illustrated by one third-century text which mentions a family group – Uricalus, his wife and two children and his brother Decentinus and his wife. All are listed as, 'The names of those who have sworn at the spring to the Goddess Sulis on the twelfth of April. Whosoever there has perjured himself you are to make him pay for it to the goddess Sulis in his own blood.' Clearly there was a family dispute in which one person was lying – the goddess would know who it was and would exact punishment.

Together these texts provide a fascinating insight into provincial life in all its pettiness, what it was that made people irate and how they relied heavily on the presiding deity to help them at every turn. For a miscreant, even if undetected, to suspect that he had been named and cursed must have been a fearsome uncertainty to live with.

Minerva, and thus presumably Sulis Minerva, had many attributes – she was a goddess of wisdom and of healing and she also possessed martial characteristics. One might expect, therefore, some indication of all this at the sacred spring. At some healing springs it was quite usual for the sick and lame to dedicate to the deity a model, usually in wood, of whatever part of their anatomy was diseased. Deposits of arms, legs, eyes and other parts have been found in France at the shrine of Sequanna at the source of the Seine and at the spring of Chamalières not far from Vichy. Bath is devoid of offerings of this type except for the single piece of ivory carved stylistically in the form of breasts (see **39**). If, however, wooden ex-votos had been thrown in they would have floated away when the sluice was open. It is sad that nothing of this kind has survived.

Of the deity's warlike attributes we have some hints. The washer from a model ballista could well have been an offering made by a soldier as thanks for some service the goddess had rendered, or in anticipation of help. That Bath was evidently popular among the army is shown by the number of military tombstones in the vicinity put up long after the garrison had moved on. Perhaps they were of soldiers who had returned to the city in their retirement to settle, or of the wounded making a pilgrimage in anticipation of a cure. We will see what kind of men they were later (Chapter 6). They would have been among the tens of thousands of people who at one time or another crowded around the three large windows in the south wall of the enclosure to see the waters, to be close to the deity and to seek her help.

The Façade of the Four Seasons

So far we have been concerned with buildings and structures whose actual sites are known. The excavations have, however, produced large quantities of building stone and sculptured blocks from other monuments sited somewhere within the precinct, otherwise unknown apart from their constituent parts. Of these, the most remarkable is the Façade of the Four Seasons, of which fourteen pieces were found in 1790, one in 1895,

another in 1968 and two more scraps in 1982. Many attempts have been made at reconstruction, but only recently have all the pieces been satisfactorily fitted into place in relation to one another (**41**).

The façade was provided with six fluted pilasters belonging to a simplified Tuscan order, dividing the wall into five spaces 1.2m (4ft) wide, the central space serving as a doorway. The other four were treated in similar ways, each being provided with a large niche roofed with a shell canopy protecting a seated figure, above which was a small recess containing a running cupid (**42**). The cupids are particularly well represented among the surviving fragments: one holding a bunch of flowers is evidently playing the part of Spring, Summer is carrying corn, Autumn holds a bunch of fruit, while Winter brandishes a billhook for cutting firewood. Of the large seated figures below, only scraps survive, but one at least, the figure below the cupid Spring, is a heavily draped female who appears to be holding a large bud over one shoulder. It seems likely that she, too, is Spring, in which case the cupids are acting out the roles of the figures below.

Immediately above the cupid recesses ran a two-line inscription, of which the section above Spring is complete. It reads, *C. Protacius ... deae Sulis Minervae*, 'Gaius Protacius ... of the goddess Sulis Minerva' – a clear reminder that the façade is closely connected with the presiding deity. Presumably the inscription was meant to be read one line at a time right across the façade. Another two-line inscription was carved on the frieze above the pilasters. Only fragments survive, but they may be translated as, 'Claudius Ligur ... excessive age ... the guild in a long sequence of years ... at its own cost had it repaired and repainted ...'. A tantalizing fragment, but sufficient to show that a building which had suffered from excessive age was repaired and repainted by a guild of craftsmen with which one Claudius Ligur was in some way associated. The building must be one of the temple structures, as the words deae Sulis Minervae imply; whether it was the temple itself or the structure to which the façade belonged will never be known.

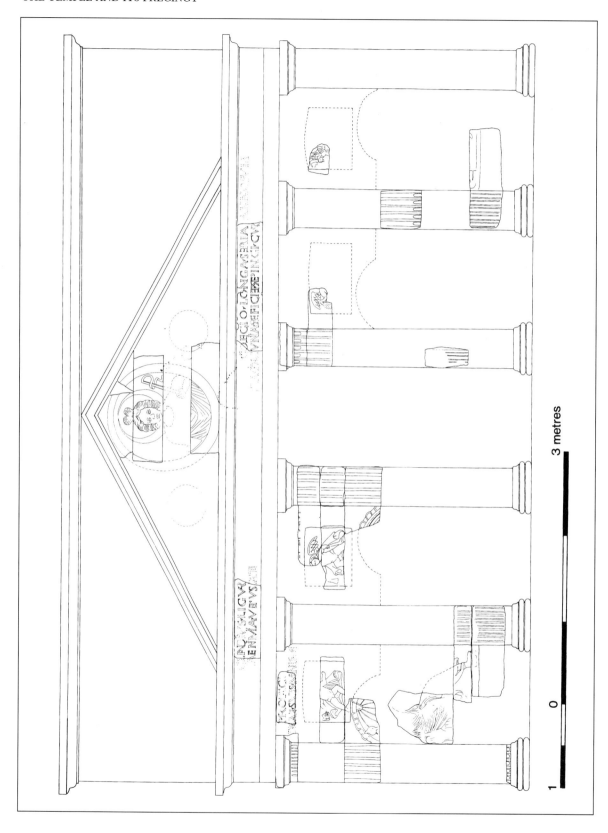

41 *Reconstruction of the Façade of the Four Seasons with the Luna pediment above.*

42 *Some of the sculptured stones found in 1790 and later belonged to a substantial monument divided into panels by fluted pilasters. Between each pair of pilasters were two niches, the lower with a shell canopy protecting a life-size seated figure, the upper depicting a cupid representing a season. (For scales see* **41**.*)*

43 *Above the Façade of the Four Seasons there was proba-bly a pediment. It may well be that the four pediment blocks found in 1790 belong to it. Together they show the goddess Luna with a crescent moon behind her head and a riding whip in one hand.*

The excavations of 1790 also produced three carved blocks belonging to a pediment 5.5m (18ft) long and 1.5m (5ft) high, carved in the centre with a roundel containing the head of the goddess Luna, shown here heavily draped with her hair piled in a high bun on the top of her head (**43**). In her hand she carries a riding whip, while behind the head, shallowly carved, is a crescent moon. The corners of the pediment appear to be enlivened with globes, but of these little survives. The style of the carving is in many ways very similar to that of the Façade of the Four Seasons, hinting that the two may belong together. In fact, when the measurements are compared, it will be seen that the pediment fits precisely over the central doorway and the two adjacent interpilaster spaces (see **41**); clearly the two elements are designed to fit the same rules of proportion and it may well be that the recon-struction offered here approximates closely to the truth. There are, of course, alternatives: for example, the façade might have belonged to a side wall while the pediment formed part of the end wall of the same building, but until the actual

foundations are located within the precinct we are unlikely ever to know.

The exact location of the monument may well never be fixed but the position in which the fallen blocks were found shows that it must have been somewhere in the vicinity of the inner precinct. The recent excavations have now removed a number of the possibilities, leaving the site north of the altar as the most reasonable guess. As we have seen, in such a location it would have neatly balanced the main portico attached to the north side of the reservoir to the south of the altar. Here the problem rests.

Monuments

Diana's hound (**44**)

One of the prize discoveries of the 1981–3 exca-vation was a fragment of a relief (in two parts) depicting a playful young hound squatting at the

44 *A lively young hound squatting at the feet of someone most likely to be the goddess Diana, whose bow can be seen above the hound's body. It was found in the temple precinct, reused as paving, in 1982. Max. height 75cm (29½in).*

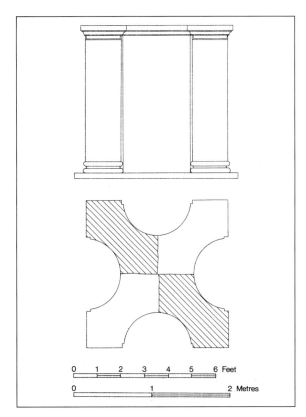

45 *Reconstruction of the niched quadrangular monument two blocks of which were found reused as paving in the temple precinct.*

feet of a draped figure and looking up at her. Part of a bow, carved just above the animal's back, leaves little doubt that we are dealing with a relief of the hunting goddess Diana. The skill of the sculptor in presenting the tensed energy of the beast is quite exceptional. It is reminiscent of several other fine animal carvings from the Bath region which may have come from the same hand or school. The nature of the monument and its location are beyond recovery: the surviving fragments were reused in a later reflooring.

The large free-standing monument (45)

Davis's excavation of 1895 produced two flat blocks which had been used at a late date as paving slabs or steps but had originally formed part of the cornice of an elaborately carved monument about 2m (6½ft) square and standing to a height of 2.4–2.8m (8–9ft). Each of the four sides

was cut to form a deep recess protecting a standing, life-size figure, but all that now remains in the top of one of the recesses is the crest of a helmet and the tip of a spear belonging to a single military personage. The external corners of the monument were simply carved to give the appearance of flanking pilasters supporting a highly decorated cornice. The quality of the work is extremely fine, but where originally the structure stood we are unlikely ever to know. It must represent one of the many monuments pulled down in the sub-Roman period and used as paving.

Dedicatory altars and other sculptures (46–8)

The temple precinct was provided with a number of lesser monuments, such as dedicatory inscriptions and small altars, which were probably tucked away in corners or against walls. Two of these, found in 1790, were both erected to the

46 *Minerva: found in the Great Bath. Height 69cm (27in).*

59

47 *Loucetius the horned god and Nemetona with three hooded figures and an animal: found in the Great Bath. Height 43cm (17in).*

48 *A triad of mother goddesses: found at Cleveland Walk. Height 24cm (9½in).*

deity Sulis for a retired centurion, Marcus Aufidius Maximus, by slaves whom he appears to have set free (p.103). Other inscriptions were put up to the goddess by Priscus, a stonemason of the Carnutes, near Chartres, and by Quintus Pompeius Anicetus. These can have formed only a few of large numbers of similar inscriptions which must have cluttered the precinct. When it is remembered that all of the monuments described above stood somewhere in the eastern half of the precinct in front of the temple, and that by the

very nature of the excavations large quantities of sculptures must still remain to be found, some idea of the ornate and densely packed atmosphere of the temple emerges. Somehow the temple authorities would have jammed in these expressions of piety, still leaving room for ritual and worship. Walking through the aisles of the abbey, only a few metres away, and looking at the closely packed dedications, it is possible to recapture something of the self-expression and parade common to both Roman and Christian religion.

4

The bathing establishment

The central bathing establishment, served by the King's Bath spring, lay immediately to the south of the temple. It was constructed in the late first century and continued in use into the late fourth or even fifth century, gradually throughout its life undergoing structural modifications, the effects of which were to improve and enlarge the facilities offered to bathers. While it is probable that alterations were continually being made, five main phases can be distinguished.

The initial layout of the baths (Period I)

The baths of the first period were (**49**) massively constructed in plain bold masonry worthy of the best contemporary work on the Continent. It would appear that the building plan was thought of as three separate units: a spacious hall, with the thermal swimming-baths to the east and a suite of artificially heated rooms to the west.

The hall was laid out about a north–south axis emphasized by screen arcades, defining the north and south sides of the central space. Each arcade was composed of massive piers supporting a wide, and proportionally higher, central arch with narrow openings on either side, and to give an added visual rigidity to the structure the piers were provided with attached pilasters which once supported an architrave and cornice. These internal arrangements were designed so as to focus attention through the north central arch on to the spring and altar beyond, which could be viewed

49 *The baths, Period I.*

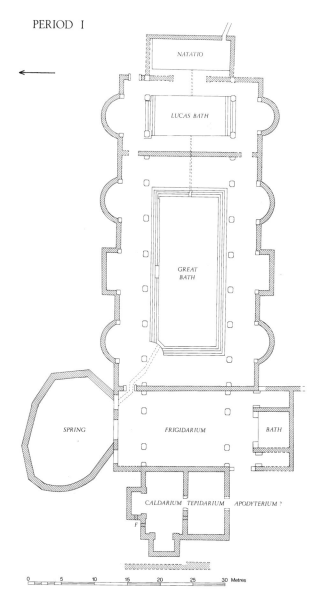

PERIOD I

NATATIO

LUCAS BATH

GREAT BATH

SPRING

FRIGIDARIUM

BATH

CALDARIUM TEPIDARIUM APODYTERIUM ?

F

0   5   10   15   20   25   30 Metres

50 *One of the square-headed windows in the north wall of the hall. A magnificent example of joggled masonry. (Scale in feet.)*

through three large windows perforating the north wall of the hall. The central arched window and the smaller square-headed window next to it with its superb joggled masonry are among the most impressive pieces of Roman architecture surviving in the country (**50, 51**). Their very simplicity was contrived to prevent distraction from the view beyond. If the structure of the northern wall of the

hall is simple to deduce, that of the southern part is far less clear, due largely to the extensive alterations to which the area was later subjected; but in broad terms a large tank or bath was provided on the central axis framed by a single arched opening, while on either side were two short passageways closed by doors for which the monolithic jambs still survive. Since the bath was a cold bath it is best to regard it, together with the hall, as the cold room (*frigidarium*) belonging to the suite of baths to the west. That access was provided in the south-west corner suggests that it is in this area, obscured by later buildings, that the main entrance lay. If no special provision had been made here for assembly and undressing then the hall itself is likely to have performed these functions.

Once in the hall, having no doubt admired the view and removed his clothes, the bather was faced with a choice. He could either turn right into the hall which housed the Great Bath, and indulge in a gentle swim in the warm water, or he could turn left towards the suite of 'Turkish' baths for a more rigorous session. The hall, then, served as a place of assembly and at the same time neatly divided the physical atmosphere of the treatments from each other.

51 *The windows in the north wall of the hall overlooking the sacred spring (see **32** and **50**).*

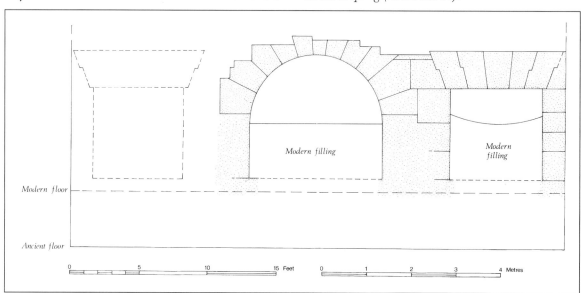

Without a doubt, the Great Bath would have been then, as it is now, one of the wonders of Roman Britain (**52**). The bath itself lay in the centre of an aisled hall 33.2m (109ft) long by 20.4m (70ft) wide, divided into a nave and two side aisles, or ambulatories, by continuous arcades framed with pilasters and entablature like those in the entrance hall. Each ambulatory was provided with three *exedrae*, a central rectangular recess with semicircular ones on either side, each framed by piers supporting arches in harmony with the main arcades. Clearly they would have formed sitting-out places for those who wished to view the bathing without getting splashed. The north-western semicircular *exedra* survived to a sufficient height to show that a large window had been set high in the centre. If all the *exedrae* had originally had windows of this kind the ambulatories would have been extremely well lighted. The hall was entered at its north-west corner from the entrance hall, through a simple opening provided with massive stone doorjambs. Stone was used because in such a steam-laden atmosphere wood would quickly have warped. Two other doors were provided, both in the east wall, to give access to a smaller swimming-bath, now known as the Lucas Bath, which lay beyond.

Occupying almost the entire central area of the chamber was the Great Bath, a basin 22 by 8.8m (72 by 29ft) sunk to a depth of 1.5m (5ft) below the floor and reached by four steep steps continuous along all four sides (**colour plate 9**). The entire sunken area was lined with sheets of lead between 1 and 2cm (⅓–¾in) thick and about 3 by 1.5m (10 by 5ft) laid in three regular rows. Originally the steps would also have been lead covered, but only a few small fragments, which could not be removed because they were wedged behind later blocks, now survive. The function of such an elaborate flooring was twofold: to keep the water in and to prevent the minor springs hereabouts from bubbling up through the bottom. The bath was fed with its main supply of water by a rectangular lead box-pipe leading into the north-west corner and linked directly to the reservoir (**53**). A culvert of similar width was provided

in the east side, through which the water passed into the Lucas Bath. For those occasions when it was necessary to drain the bath, or otherwise to regulate the flow, a sluice in the north-east corner could be brought into use to drain water into the main outfall. When the baths were first uncovered, Davis records that this drain was fitted with a bronze sluice, which has since been removed and is now in the museum.

In the general austerity of the hall only a single ornamental feature was provided in the form of a fountain or similar structure set in the centre of the north side of the bath, though it is a distinct possibility that the semicircular arrangement in the north-west corner of the bath, at the point where the water enters the bath, was also in some way adorned, perhaps with statuary.

In their original state the ambulatories which surrounded the Great Bath were floored with massive slabs of hard white lias limestone, about 20cm (8in) thick, most of which are still excellently preserved. Where a considerable volume of water dripping from the bathers would have accumulated on the paving around the edge of the bath between the piers, shallow gutters were cut into the paving, returning at their ends to the edge of the bath to channel the water back.

While we can describe in some detail the ground-plan of the various features, assessment of the superstructure is much more difficult, but the fortunate chance that so much of the collapsed building has survived in the mud allows the general form, if not the detail, of the upper part of the hall to be reconstructed. The spacing and size of the arcade piers and of their attached pilasters demand that the framing entablature, which the pilasters supported, should be at a maximum height of 7.3m (24ft) above the ambulatory (**54**). This much is certain and substantial parts of the entablature, found in the rubble, allow total reconstruction thus far. What happened above is much less clear, but since the general proportions of the room would require a ceiling at a height of about 13.7m (45ft) or more to prevent a claustrophobic feeling, there must have been another stage above the lower entablature and moreover a stage which included large lunettes to

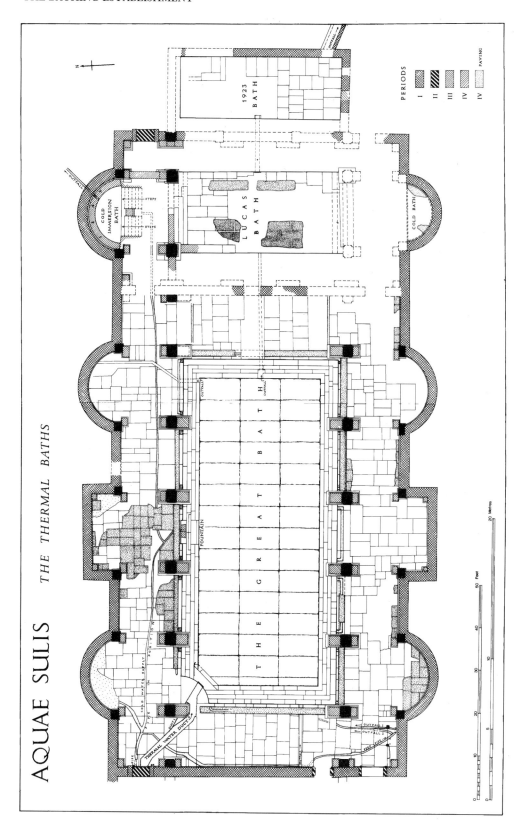

52 *The Great Bath.*

1 *Gilded bronze head of Minerva.*

2 *The temple precinct towards the end of the excavation.*
3 *Excavations in progress in the sacred spring.*

4 *Reconstruction of the spring as it may have been in the third century.*

JOHN RONAYNE

5 *Gemstones found in the sacred spring.*

6 *Finds from the sacred spring.*

7 *The terminals of a bronze penannular brooch from the sacred spring, inset with red enamel.*

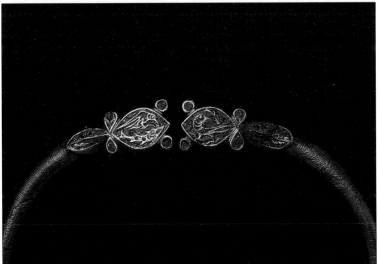

8 *Curse scratched on a sheet of pewter from the sacred spring.*

9 *The Great Bath.*

smaller room into which was tightly fitted another bath, measuring 11.9 by 4.4m (39 by 14½ft), discovered by Knowles in 1923. Although it has never been completely excavated, an area of the original stone paving can still be seen in position and in the north-east corner, now refilled, steps were found leading up to the main floor level. One small fragment of lead still in position shows that this, too, was originally lined with lead. Water was provided by the culvert leading in from the Lucas Bath, while the main outfall led from the south-east corner. Visually the Lucas Bath and 1923 bath functioned together, the 1923 bath appearing simply as a basin in an alcove opening out of the side of the Lucas Bath chamber. The opening was probably framed by a simple arch set behind an engaged entablature in the manner of the main hall. While the Lucas Bath would have been roofed in the same way as the Great Bath, the 1923 bath may well have been enclosed with a lower ceiling probably on the level of the main entablature. Thus the thermal bath range consisted of swimming-baths decreasing in size, grandeur and temperature.

Returning now to the other end of the establishment, the heated baths on the west side of the hall were altogether different in function and architecture. The rooms were smaller and each was designed for a specific purpose. It seems likely that access to the suite was provided from the hall by means of a southern corridor (now obscured by later features), from which the bather would normally pass into the adjacent *tepidarium* (warm room). Although the *tepidarium* was later refloored at a higher level, the general arrangement in the first period must have been much the same as it later became, with hot air coming in through vents in the north wall, into a basement created by supporting the main floor on regularly spaced piers of tiles (*pilae*). After circulating in this space the air passed into a jacketing of vertical box-tiles attached to the walls of the room, which led out through chimneys in the roof. The rising of the hot air through the wall flues created the draught necessary to draw more hot air into the basement hypocaust, thus maintaining the flow.

The later floor of this room incorporated the further refinement of hollow box-tile jacketing within the thickness of the floor. Such an arrangement would have made a far more efficient use of the hot air but we cannot be certain that the same system was employed in the first period.

Through a wide door in the north wall of the *tepidarium* lay the *caldarium* (hot room), of similar size. Although the drastic remodelling of the fourth period has completely destroyed the original fittings, there can be little doubt that the floor would have been constructed in much the same way as that of the *tepidarium*, with the hot air supplied by a flue opening through the north wall. The room was provided with two large recesses, each of which was fitted out with small plunge baths heated from below and no doubt served with hot water from a boiler above the main stokery to the north.

The use of these rooms is clear. Having first undressed, probably in the hall, the bather would have entered the *tepidarium*, a room of gentle heat designed to prepare the body for more vigorous treatment. After a while he would have passed into the hot steamy atmosphere of the *caldarium*, where he could choose between sitting in the main room or bathing in the hot plunges provided in the alcoves. It may well be that these were so arranged that one was hotter than the other, allowing the bather to work up gradually to the hottest treatment. When the spell in the 'Turkish' bath was over, the body would be allowed to cool off gradually by passing slowly through the *tepidarium*. Finally, the treatment would be completed with a swim in the cold bath set in the alcove in the south side of the hall.

No certain evidence survives as to the nature of the roof of this part of the building. There would have been no need for the high spaces provided for the thermal baths to the east where height was a positive advantage to allow the steam from the thermal water to rise. In the heated range quite the reverse was true, as relatively low ceilings would have been required to retain the hot, steamy atmosphere. Since wooden structures were quite useless in baths of this kind (the wood

allow sidelight into the chamber. The only fragments of architecture which could have belonged to
this second stage are several sections of engaged
half columns, again found by Davis within the rubble filling the hall. One reasonable explanation is
that engaged columns were used above the pilasters
in the second stage to echo the framing of the lower
stage. If so, they would have divided the wall into a
series of panels between which would have been
semicircular-headed lunettes matching in proportion
the lower arcade. Such an arrangement would have
been most effective, as the reconstruction shows: in
general conception it was not at all unlike contemporary buildings in Rome, such as the Colosseum.

The roofing of the ambulatories is a much simpler problem. A ceiling with a pitched roof above
could easily have been provided on the level of
the lower entablature, while the *exedrae* would
have been separately treated. The wall surfaces
were simply plastered with a thick red mortar
which originally would have been painted in
areas of plain colour.

It will be apparent from the foregoing discussion that the chamber containing the Great Bath
was a considerable architectural achievement. Its
lines were bold and clean-cut – it was above all a
functional building admirably designed to fulfil
its purpose. For effect it depended entirely upon
the imposing solidity of its masonry and the careful use of volumes and light. No one entering the
hall for the first time could have failed to have
been impressed by its simple majesty.

Beyond the east wall of the main hall was a
smaller chamber, 20.4m (67ft) long by 10.4m
(34ft) wide, containing the Lucas Bath, first discovered in 1755. Strictly, it was a continuation of
the basic structure of the main hall, but its visual
axis, like that of the entrance hall, was
north–south. In the centre lay the bath, 13.1 by
c. 6.1m (43ft by *c.* 20ft), reached by flights of five
steps arranged along the two short sides between
the piers. Presumably, like the Great Bath, it
would have been lead lined, but later refloorings
have removed all trace. The water supply
entered the west side through a culvert connected with the Great Bath and waste water was

53 *The hot mineral water straight from the reservoir
entered the Great Bath at its north-west corner over a quad-
rant-shaped projection which may once have supported an
ornamental feature.*

allowed to drain out of the east side by means of
a similar vent leading into yet another bath. The
two semicircular recesses with which the ends of
the hall were enlivened were probably, like those
of the Great Bath, fitted out for relaxing, but
later alterations have obliterated the earliest
arrangement.

The centre of the east wall of the Lucas Bath
was pierced by a wide opening leading into a

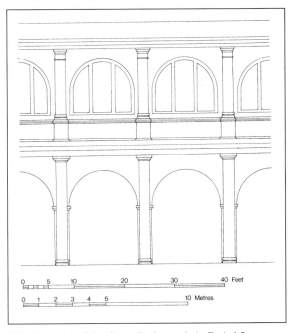

54 *Elevation of the Great Bath arcade in Period I.*

12 *The sanctuary and adjacent buildings enclosed by a wall in the fourth century.*

10 *The strengthened piers of the Great Bath hall.*

11 *Reconstruction of the bathing establishment in the third century.*

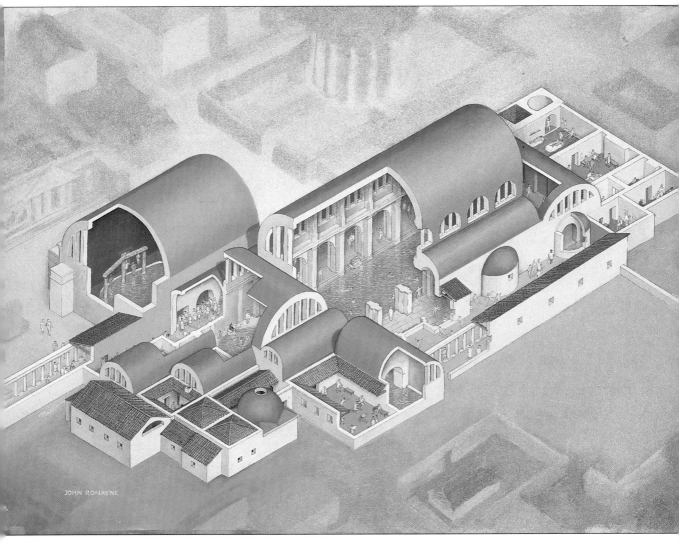

JOHN RONAYNE

would have warped and there would have been constant danger from fire), the two heated rooms must have been vaulted with concrete and box-tiles, presumably in two parallel east–west tunnel vaults. It will never be known whether the vaults were left as bare concrete, as they were in the famous Hunting Baths at Lepcis Magna (Libya), or if they were covered with pitched slated roofs, rather more suitable for a rainy climate. The side corridors were, however, almost certainly covered with simple pitched roofs.

As we have shown, it is possible to describe the original bathing establishment in considerable detail, not only as a ground-plan but also in terms of its function and superstructure. It remains to say something of its date. On archaeological grounds there is very little evidence. A limited excavation south of the entrance hall produced a few fragments of late first- or early second-century pottery from a lens of soil which had accumulated over the building spread contemporary with the initial construction, suggesting the possibility of a late first-century date, but this is hardly conclusive. Nor can much be said on architectural grounds. The style of the building in its bold simplicity defies accurate dating, but it would not have been out of place in late first-century Rome, where several buildings in a similar vein were being erected. The inscriptions found in Bath from time to time throw some light on the problem. Several of them, put up by visitors to the spa, are of first-century date and, since people are unlikely to have made the journey to visit a bubbling marsh, the implication is that the baths were in existence at this time. Finally, it is to the late first century that the first series of massive monumental urban building in Britain belongs. Civic authorities were receiving official encouragement from the government for their building programmes – Bath may have been one of them.

The first extension to the bathing establishment (Period II)

At a time not long after the original building was put up, major alterations were undertaken at both the east and west ends to improve the range of facilities offered to bathers (**55**). At the east end the 1923 bath and its alcove were dismantled and the inlet which fed it from the Lucas Bath was joined to the outlet by a stone-built culvert running diagonally across the bath: it can still be seen in a tolerably well-preserved state. Having thus rearranged the drainage system the old bath was filled with rubble; its original walls were thickened by new internal foundations, the added strength being needed to support the heavy vaulted superstructure. Further extensions were made to the south and east. The resulting suite was very much like the arrangement of the early 'Turkish' baths at the west end.

The visitor, entering through a small door in the south-east corner of the Lucas Bath chamber, would find himself in a pair of gently warmed rooms leading to a large 6m (20ft) square undressing room. Returning through the passage he would enter the *tepidarium*, built over the old 1923 bath, warmed to a higher temperature by means of hot air entering the hypocausts from the *caldarium* to the north. As soon as he was acclimatized he would have proceeded into the *caldarium*, a rectangular room with a large semicircular bath opening from one wall. The high temperature of the room was maintained by a massive flue immediately to the north, which produced both the hot air circulating beneath the floor and a plentiful supply of hot water from a boiler which would have been constructed over the flue. At the end of the steam treatment he would have cooled his body gradually by passing through the *tepidarium*, probably completing the session with a gentle swim in the tepid water of the Lucas Bath before returning to the changing room.

The superstructure of the new baths is easy to reconstruct theoretically. The range of heated rooms, and probably the flue as well, would have been covered with a simple barrel vault arranged on a north–south axis, while the semicircular bath of the *caldarium* would have been provided with a semi-dome. The undressing room and the passage to the south were probably protected by a pitched roof.

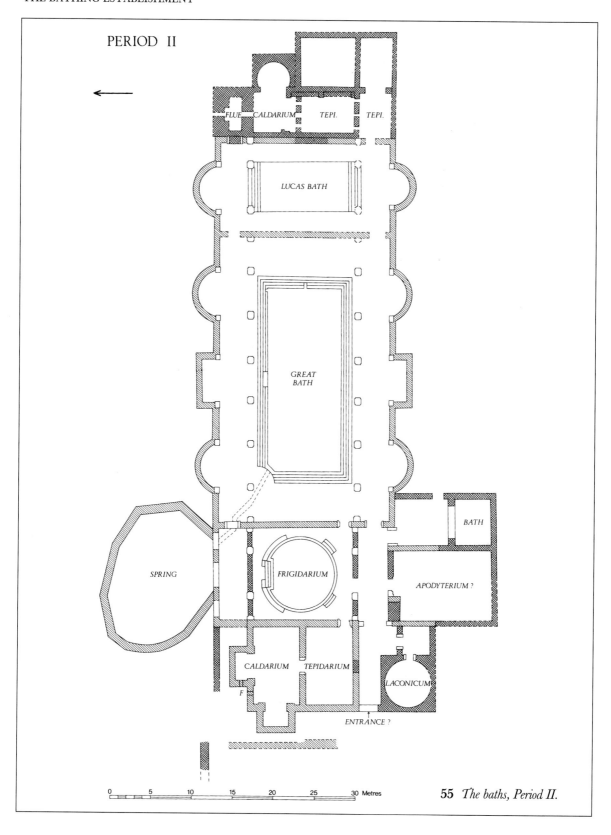

PERIOD II

FLUE CALDARIUM TEPI. TEPI.

LUCAS BATH

GREAT
BATH

BATH

SPRING

FRIGIDARIUM

APODYTERIUM ?

CALDARIUM TEPIDARIUM

LACONICUM

F

ENTRANCE ?

0   5   10   15   20   25   30 Metres

55 *The baths, Period II.*

The alterations at the west end were altogether more far-reaching (**56**), but, simply stated, a new type of bathing facility was inserted into the area between the Great Bath and the eastern range of 'Turkish' baths. The central element of the new treatment was a large circular room known as a *laconicum*, which would have been heated by means of a flue in the south wall to a very high temperature indeed. Since it was *dry* heat that was required, the *laconicum* was isolated from the rest of the baths to prevent contamination from the general steamy atmosphere. Next to it a large court was created by

the obliteration of the first-period bath and corridors, south of the entrance hall, and by further extension to the south. The newly defined area was paved with large slabs of limestone. Its function is uncertain. While it is most likely to have been an undressing room (*apodyterium*), the possibility that it may have been an exercise court should not be ruled out. It was conveniently placed, opening off the main east–west corridor which would have led from the main entrance at the west end of

56 *The west baths.*

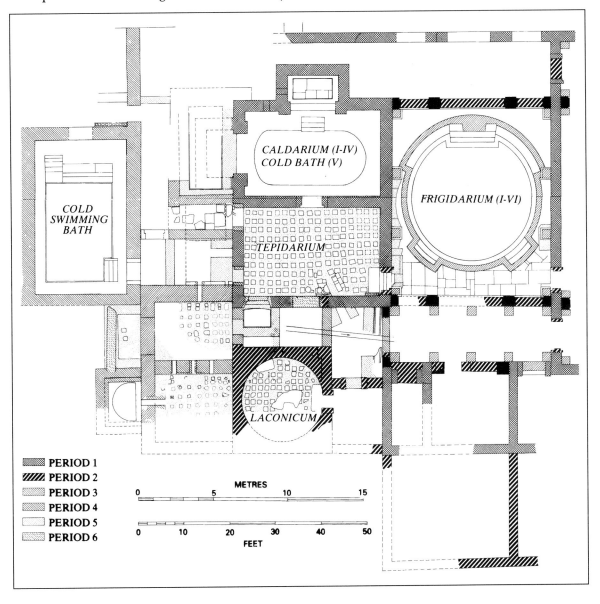

PERIOD 1
PERIOD 2
PERIOD 3
PERIOD 4
PERIOD 5
PERIOD 6

COLD SWIMMING BATH

CALDARIUM (I-IV)
COLD BATH (V)

FRIGIDARIUM (I-VI)

TEPIDARIUM

LACONICUM

METRES
0   5   10   15

FEET
0   10   20   30   40   50

the establishment to a new doorway cut in the west wall of the Great Bath chamber.

The third element of the new arrangement consisted of a circular plunge bath nearly 9m (30ft) in diameter and 1.2m (4ft) deep, which was fitted rather tightly into the central area of the entrance hall. The bath was provided with steps of massive masonry leading down from the surrounding paved area to its floor, which originally was probably of lead-covered stone flags, but now only the rubble foundation survives. Into the north side of the bath projects a platform which would once have supported an ornamental fountain supplying cold water. The overflow can still be seen leading out of the south-east corner into an extensive series of sewers which eventually drain into a culvert running along the south side of the establishment into the main drain.

Alterations as extensive as these necessarily caused a displacement and reorganization of the other facilities. The old hall, now containing the Circular Bath, was walled across between the arcade piers on the north and south sides. With the exception of a single doorway in the south, the walls were probably taken up to fill the arcades completely. This would have meant that the view across the spring was now destroyed, but it is a distinct possibility that the corridor to the north of the Circular Bath was refloored at a higher level to serve as a viewing platform for the spring, reached by steps from the north ambulatory of the Great Bath or direct from the temple precinct. In fact, much the same as the present arrangement. An interesting piece of evidence to support this suggestion is that the north-facing sides of the two piers were enlivened with fluting (57), which stops not at the original first-period floor but at the new platform level with which the tooling is likely to be contemporary. Clearly the view *into* the baths from the temple was important.

Additional access to the baths was now provided through a new entrance hall attached to the south-west corner of the Great Bath chamber, which opened into what was originally the south-west corner of the old hall but was now a passageway linking various elements of the

57 *The piers in the entrance hall were massive. Those which would have been seen by someone looking into the hall from the temple precinct were fluted. (Scale in feet.)*

establishment. The new entrance hall was provided with a large bath opening out of the south wall and replacing functionally the closely similar bath that was filled up to make way for the *apodyterium*. The whole area is now heavily cluttered with derelict machinery and rubbish, but nevertheless some limited excavation was possible. This showed that the bath was originally floored with large limestone flagstones which had later been covered with a thick coating of red mortar continuous with the rendering of the walls and steps leading to it. It is very much to be hoped that one day the whole of this important area will be cleared and put on display. Why a subsidiary entrance should have been provided here is not immediately apparent, but one explanation is that it provided access to an exercise yard south of the Great Bath.

and quite probably the upper, would not have looked very different – the same proportions and detailing could easily have been retained in front of a greatly strengthened substructure (**61**). The main difference lay in the nature of the roof itself, for the original ceiling, presumably of coffered timberwork, was now replaced by a somewhat higher concrete vault open at both ends to allow the steam to escape. Large fragments of the vault found within the rubble filling the bath show that it was constructed of hollow box-tiles, to reduce the weight, capped with a covering of concrete and tiles. The ends of the vault were framed with large semicircular lunettes. Part of one, which still survives and is displayed in the baths (**62**), was neatly finished with a tiled facing to the *intrados* with horizontally coursed tiles filling the space between the lunette and the vault.

The haunches of the main vault rested on the arcades which, as we have seen, were strengthened to take the greatly increased vertical thrusts. Since the ambulatory would have been roofed with continuous tunnel vaults at normal ceiling level or a little higher, the lateral thrusts to which the piers were subjected would have been dissipated by the buttressing effect of the ambulatory structure. Further buttressing was provided by the *exedrae*. The beautiful simplicity of the whole structural concept is shown best by the section (see **61**).

While there is no doubt that the vault of the Great Bath lay east–west, the arrangement over the Lucas Bath is a little less certain. Strictly, it could have been vaulted with a continuation of the main vault, but the strengthening of the north–south walls of the chamber, with supports for blind arcades, is a strong indication that in

59 *The Great Bath empty of water showing the sheets of lead lining the bottom. The modern colonnaded ambulatory does not reproduce in any way the original Roman appearance.*

60 *To strengthen the side walls of the Great Bath when the vaulted roof was built, additional piers were added to absorb the lateral thrust. (Scale in feet.)*

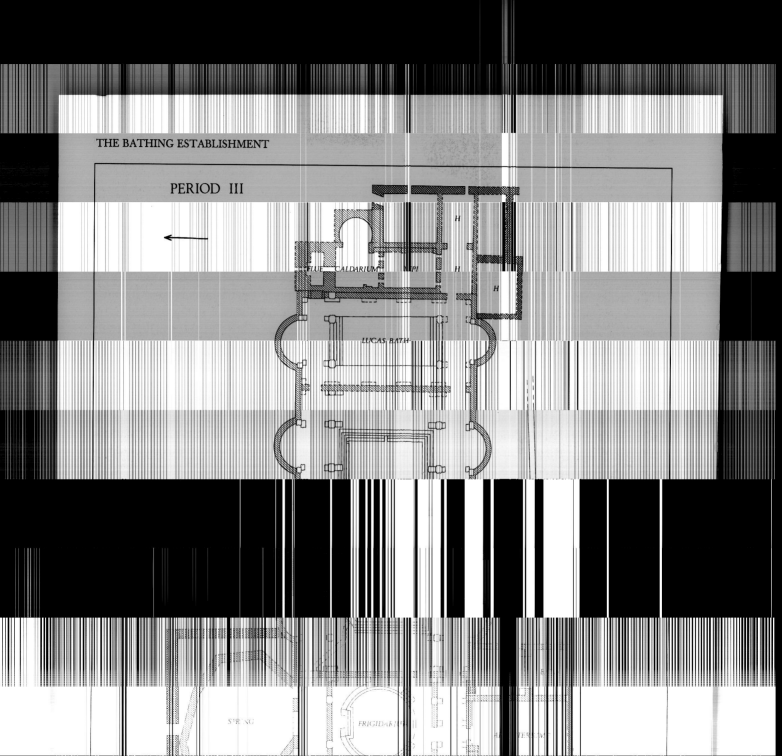

THE BATHING ESTABLISHMENT

PERIOD III

←

FLUE CALDARIUM *HPI*

H

H

H

LUCAS BATH

SPRING FRIGIDARIUM

Having described the extensive additions and alterations, we must now consider how the new suite was intended to function. After undressing in the *apodyterium*, it is likely that the exercise was taken to tone up the muscles and produce a pleasant tiredness. Then the bather would enter the *laconicum*, sitting first of all low down and gradually (if the facility were provided) moving to a higher tier of seats where the atmosphere would be much hotter. The *laconicum* functioned, in fact, in exactly the same way as a modern Scandinavian sauna bath, the intense dry heat of the bath promoting profuse sweating. A period in the enervating atmosphere would be immediately followed by a sharp plunge in the cold water of the Circular Bath. Finally, the bather could choose between returning to the entrance hall to dress or a gentle swim in the warm water of the Great Bath before finally emerging from the establishment.

It will be evident from the plan that the construction of the 'sauna' baths cut off the access to the western range of 'Turkish' baths. To overcome this difficulty, two new doors were cut in the east and west walls of the Circular Bath chamber, thus providing a direct route between the Great Bath and the *tepidarium*. A bather wishing to take a 'Turkish bath', on entering and changing, would proceed through to the chamber containing the Circular Bath to the *tepidarium* and eventually the *caldarium* before returning to the Circular Bath for a cold dip. Thus the Circular Bath now served as the cold plunge for both sauna and Turkish treatments.

The exact date at which these changes took place is difficult to define and indeed we cannot be certain that they were all of one period, but the similarity of the masonry at both the east and west ends suggests that both sets of alterations are broadly contemporary and the fact that the *laconicum* is detached hints at a date no later than the middle of the second century. Of the few scraps of pottery found beneath the contemporary building spread on the south side of the baths, none dates to after the first quarter of the second century. Therefore the evidence, such as it is, would allow the alterations to have taken place during the reign of Hadrian.

To summarize the whole range of second-period alterations, it may be said that they were designed to enlarge greatly the facilities offered to the public. In addition to the original thermal swimming-baths and range of 'Turkish' baths, a second set of 'Turkish' baths was added, together with the rather more specialized 'sauna' baths. Why two 'Turkish' establishments were required is not clear. One possibility is that instead of opening at different times for males and females, as was frequently the practice at this time, the establishment was now rearranged so that both sexes could use the building at the same time. By closing the door between the Circular Bath and *tepidarium*, the western 'Turkish' baths could have been completely isolated from the rest of the establishment, thus maintaining propriety. The theory, however possible, must remain completely speculative.

Rebuilding and reroofing (Period III)

At some stage during the late second or early third century the decision was taken to extend the establishment and to reroof it completely (**58**), probably because the original timber roof, which by this time might well have been about a hundred years old, had warped and rotted in the damp atmosphere. The answer was to reroof entirely with masonry with an enormous barrel vault sprung from the side arcades. Such a project necessarily entailed the considerable strengthening of the supporting foundations and the creation of buttressing masses to absorb the newly created lateral thrusts. The foundations are fortunately so well preserved that the details of the work can be closely followed.

In the hall containing the Great Bath the arcade piers were considerably strengthened by cutting back the base moulds of the engaged pilasters and extending them by adding new bases to the front and back (**59, colour plate 10**). The external walls of the chamber were also strengthened with new piers added to those which framed the alcoves and by the addition of further piers to the inner angles of the rectangular alcoves (**60**). Although superficially the new work might be thought to alter the internal appearance of the hall, the lower stage,

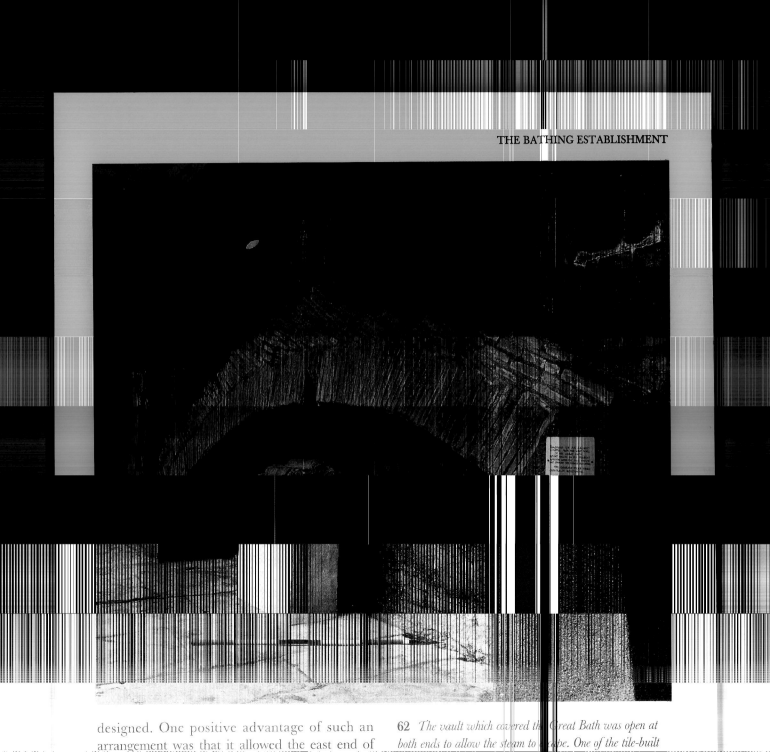

designed. One positive advantage of such an
arrangement was that it allowed the east end of

62 *The vault which covered the Great Bath was open at
both ends to allow the steam to escape. One of the tile-built*

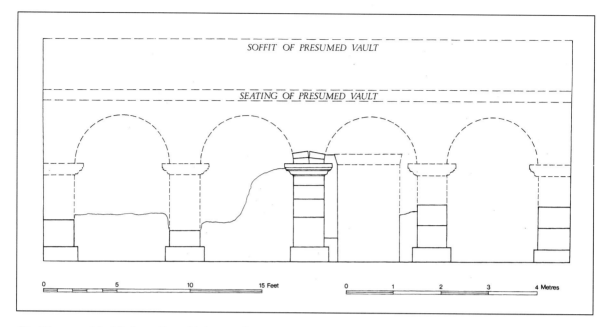

SOFFIT OF PRESUMED VAULT

SEATING OF PRESUMED VAULT

63 *Diagram of the blind arcading added south of the Circular Bath to strengthen the walls.*

The effect of these third-period alterations was to enclose completely the central elements of the bathing establishment with masonry. The skilful use of blind arcading to thicken the load-bearing walls caused minimum disruption to the existing superstructure: as far as possible the new features were constructed within the shell of the old without large-scale demolition. But in spite of the careful planning, the central part of the baths must have been out of commission for a considerable time while the vault was being erected. Enormous amounts of timber shuttering and scaffolding would have been required to build the frame over which the vaults were laid, completely choking the baths. It would have remained for some time while the concrete was setting, until the architect in charge finally took the decision to remove it. It must have been an agonizing period to live through: waiting to see if the calculations had been correct and the materials strong enough, as the whole structure settled together in a new complex of carefully balanced thrusts and tensions.

At about the same time alterations were being carried out on the heated baths at both ends. At the east end the changing room of the earlier period and the smaller room to the south were completely remodelled. The east wall was rebuilt on a more massive scale and both rooms were now provided with hypocausts heated by means of flues opening through the east wall. At least two more heated rooms were now added to the south. The general effect of these changes was to increase the number of *caldaria* in which the bathers could sweat profusely before swimming in the curative waters of the Great Bath or Lucas Bath. Thus it was the curative facilities of the baths that were now being extended. The rebuilding of the east wall on a more massive scale is an interesting indication that now that the easternmost range of rooms was heated, it was thought desirable to replace its roof with a vault to reduce the hazard of fire.

Alterations and additions were also being undertaken to the south of the Great Bath. The second-period entrance way into the south-east corner of the old entrance hall was now blocked up and various minor additions were made to the bath which opened out of the south wall of the second-period hall. Clearly these rooms were no longer a functional part of the ranges to the north. It is, however, a distinct possibility that they now formed part of a new south range,

about which practically nothing is known, perhaps linked to the southwards extension of the east baths described above. Between these two southward projections runs a stylobate of massive stone blocks supporting a full-scale colonnade, some of the bases of which still survive in position. The columns would have taken a sloping veranda roof resting against a wall to the south. While it is likely that this constituted the entire structure hereabouts, the southern wall being the limit of the establishment, it is just possible that what we are seeing is the north-facing veranda of a large, as yet undefined, building to the south. Only further excavation will provide the answers.

One interesting change took place at a later date: the bases of the columns were cut back and a series of curious massively framed window mouldings were inserted between them, serving to isolate the veranda from the open area to the north. One of the mouldings still survives in position.

At the west end there were further modifications. It seems that the main entrance was resited between the *laconicum* and *apodyterium* so that a suite of three new heated rooms could be built abutting the west wall of the establishment. The central room, opening directly from the access corridor, may have been little more than a heated lobby serving the other two. The room to the north was provided with a small sunken heated bath and it is quite possible that the southern room was similarly fitted out. The facility is clearly additional to those already provided at the west end and it is tempting to see it as the first suite of curative

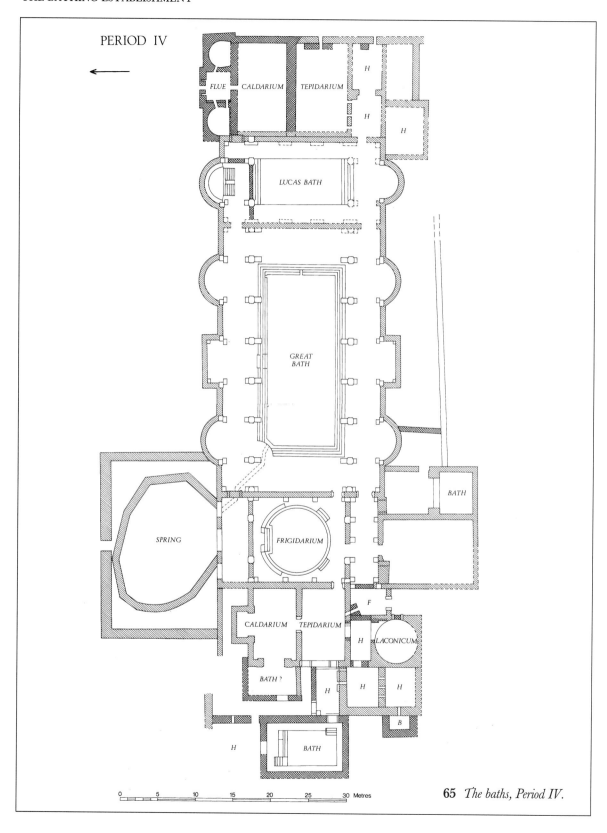

PERIOD IV

FLUE

CALDARIUM

TEPIDARIUM

H

H

H

LUCAS BATH

GREAT
BATH

BATH

SPRING

FRIGIDARIUM

F

CALDARIUM

TEPIDARIUM

H

LACONICUM

BATH ?

H

H

H

H

B

H

BATH

0   5   10   15   20   25   30 Metres

65 *The baths, Period IV.*

The reorganization of the bathing facilities (Period IV) (65 and colour plate 11)

The reorganization following some years after the great period of reroofing was on a very large scale (**65, colour plate 11**), creating at the east end the most impressive suite of heated rooms ever to be built at Bath (**66**). This was accomplished quite simply by demolishing the *tepidarium*, *caldarium* and flue of the second period, which had served until now, and replacing them

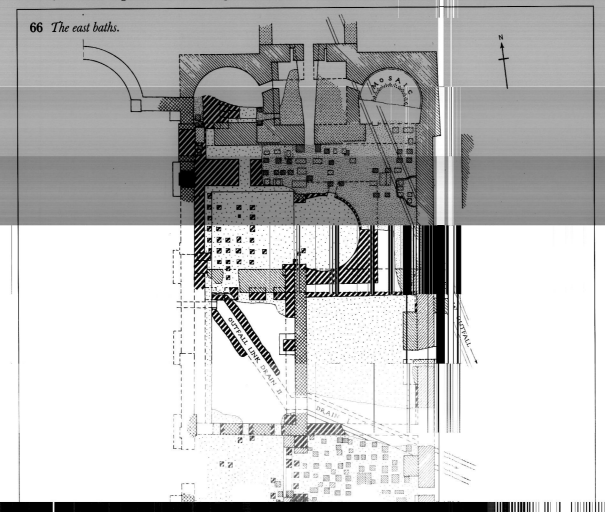

66 *The east baths.*

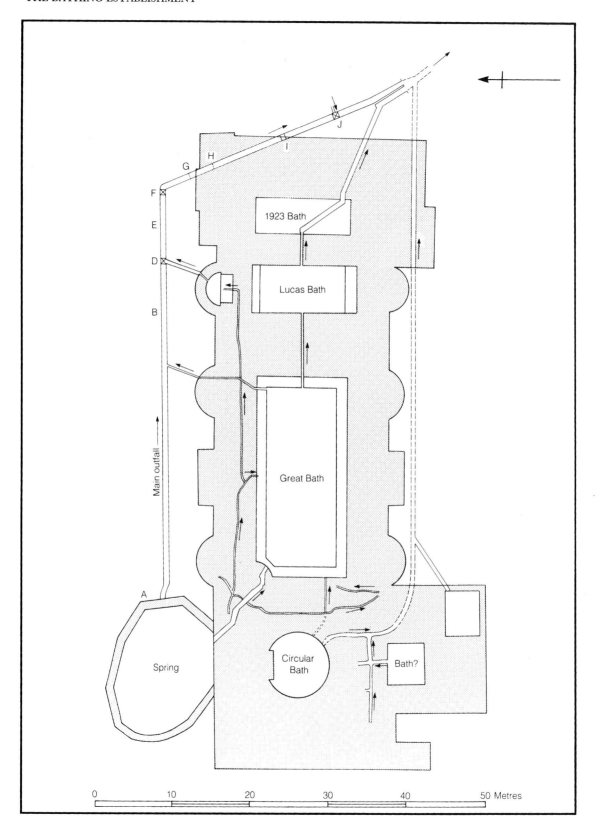

1923 Bath

Lucas Bath

Great Bath

Main outfall

Spring

Circular Bath

Bath?

A B C D E F G H I J

0   10   20   30   40   50 Metres

67 *Diagram to show the drains and water supply of the baths.*

with two vast new rooms measuring 6.7 by 11.3m (22 by 37ft). The southern room, which functioned as a *tepidarium*, was without internal elaborations, but the northern room, the *caldarium*, was fitted with a pair of fine semicircular baths floored with simple mosaic pavements. Between them was a large flue for providing the hot air for the hypocaust of the *caldarium* itself as well as for the hypocausts below the semicircular baths. It was these floors that the antiquarians of 1755 were recording, but very little survived the construction of the Kingston Baths.

The chamber containing the Lucas Bath underwent a series of interesting alterations at about this time. The northern alcove was walled off from the main room and made accessible only from the north ambulatory of the Great Bath. The floor of the alcove was then considerably lowered and a new floor laid at a depth of 1.2m (4ft) with a stone bench around the curve of the apse. The floor was reached by a flight of steps from the centre of which projected a stone culvert supplying water. The purpose of the new arrangement is clear: the alcove was converted into a curative immersion bath in which the patient sat immersed up to the neck in the healing water. Treatment of this kind was popular in Rome ever since the Emperor Augustus was cured in this way (in 23 BC) by the physician Antonius Musa.

The water for the new bath was provided directly from the sacred spring through a lead pipe which ran along the bottom of the Great Bath. A branch from a leadmain on the north side. This lead pipe is still remarkably preserved in much of its length and the channel in which it lay can be traced as a slot cut into the stone slabs (68). It was probably inserted at the same

chamber was also provided with a sunken bath lined with waterproof pink mortar. Although it is impossible to be sure when the change was made, it could be broadly of this period.

At the west end far-reaching alterations were also being undertaken. A totally new cold plunge bath was built, immediately adjacent to the existing baths beyond the west wall. It was associated with a new suite of heated rooms, to the north, about which little is known because they lie beneath an unexcavated part of Stall Street. To reach this new facility access had to be extensively reorganized, the original Period I *tepidarium* now serving as a heated vestibule. One doorway led

68 *The ambulatories surrounding the Great Bath were paved with slabs of limestone 20cm (8in) thick. Late in the life of the establishment a new lead water-pipe was inserted in a slot cut into the slabs and a new paving was laid above. The lead pipe and patch of the second floor still survive. (Scale in feet.)*

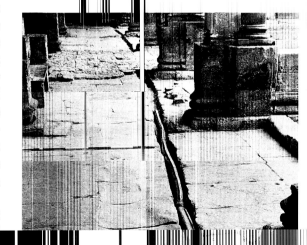

69 *The west baths after Major Davis's 1886 douche and massage baths had been removed and before the new office building was erected above. The hypocaust of the main* tepidarium *is well preserved.*

through another heated corridor direct to the new cold plunge: another gave access to a narrow corridor leading to the new heated suite, while a third, in the south wall, opened into a heated vestibule leading to the rooms added in Period III and also, through a new door, to the *laconicum.* These complexities are best appreciated by reference to the plan (see **56**). At the same time all the earlier hypocausts were gutted and rebuilt at a higher level, the old *tepidarium* (**69**) was provided with a new flue in its south wall, a small hot bath was added to the Period III heated room and the west bath of the old *caldarium* was completely rebuilt.

The overall effect of this extensive refurbishment at the west end was greatly to extend the facilities but since the entire plan has not yet been recovered it is difficult to appreciate the underlying logic of the arrangement. For the bather, however, the maze of corridors and plethora of doors must have been more than a little confusing.

The final alterations (Periods V and VI)

It was in the fifth period that the western baths reached their final form. The old *caldarium*, which had served from Period I, was now dismantled and an oval-ended oblong swimming-bath was inserted to serve as a cold bath (70). The little bath attached to the north side now also became a cold pool while the warm bath in the west alcove was walled across and now opened only to

70 *The west baths (with part of Major Davis's baths still in position). The oval-ended cold bath was inserted into the original* caldarium *the west alc . . . the establishment.*

bath was added to the south . . . . The small baths attached to the heated rooms west of the *laconicum* were also refitted.

Although these alterations were comparatively minor, and were undertaken without dislocating the superstructure, the loss of the *caldarium* must

At the east end changes were altogether more drastic. It seems that the hypocaust basements were now suffering from periods of flooding (pp.115–17) and to counteract this the basement floor levels were raised by about 22cm (8½in) with puddled clay rammed between the *pilae*. Though superficially of a minor nature, the work would have entailed the removal of all suspended floors and their subsequent replacement. At about this time, the flue was partly blocked to support a new hot-water boiler, which meant that the semicircular baths could no longer be heated direct from the flue. Provision had to be made, therefore, to provide hot air from the *caldarium*. In a final sixth phase, the hypocaust at the south end of the east baths was finally abandoned, the room being refloored with hard pink mortar.

These are the last definable alterations before the flooding became so serious that the establishment had to be abandoned, and the centre of Bath reverted once more to a marsh.

5
Aquae Sulis: spa or town?

In the two preceding chapters we have looked in some detail at the temple and the thermal baths – the two buildings which together formed the core of the Roman curative establishment. They are remarkable both for their monumental scale and for the extent of their preservation, but we must remember that they form only part of a far more extensive complex of buildings which clustered around the springs. Before we can begin to consider the question raised in the chapter title we must look at some of the other structures which made up the Roman settlement. Beyond the temple and the main baths our knowledge is still very incomplete. Even so, sufficient has come to light to produce some useful insights.

The tholos

Immediately to the east of the temple and north of the bathing establishment massive Roman foundations were exposed when the Concert Room was constructed in 1897. Fortunately the walls were carefully planned by Richard Mann. More recent work, in 1991, has added further details and it now appears that there were at least three parallel north–south walls of massive proportions each terminating in a substantial pier base set in an east–west retaining wall. A possible continuation of the east–west wall was noted 20m (66ft) to the east during work on the

monumental character and was constructed on a carefully levelled terrace.

Comparison with Gaulish sites suggests two possibilities: either it was part of a great forum and basilica arrangement, or it was the stage area of a theatre. In Gaul both types of buildings were frequently found in central positions arranged adjacent to, and on the same axis as, large temples. Architecturally neither would be out of context here in Bath but it must be admitted that there is no structural evidence to allow positive identification and the proximity of the abbey rules out decisive excavation.

A further possibility is that the foundations represent a monumental precinct containing another temple. Of direct relevance to the discussion are a number of sculpted blocks found scattered immediately south of the foundations during the excavation of the baths between 1878 and 1882. Four, all belonging to a circular monument, are of particular interest. One is part of an architrave, the other two belong to the frieze (71). All four are elaborately carved back and front in a style that can best be compared with northern Gaulish workmanship of the early second century best paralleled in the baths at Sens in northern France. From the same general area were recovered two fragments of Corinthian capitals and a part of a plain column consisting of a base and three sec-

71 *Several blocks carved with elaborate motifs, found in the rubble filling the baths, constitute part of a circular building, probably a shrine, which may have stood in the courtyard east of the temple precinct. The frieze has a continuous tendril motif on the inner face, while the outer face is carved in panels containing human figures and floral designs. Height 46cm (18in).*

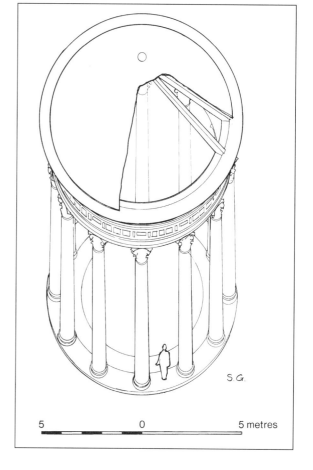

72 *The tholos as it might have been.*

Sufficient of the entablature survives to show that the circular monument (or tholos) of which they formed a part was c. 9.1m (30ft) in diameter – almost exactly the same as the width of the front of the main temple. A consideration of the decorative arrangement on the face of the frieze suggests columns c. 0.6m (2ft) in diameter at the top. This would be consistent with the size of the plain column found nearby and suggests that the columns would have been c. 7.2m (24ft) high. Given their proportions there are likely to have been 12 columns. Once again, as with other monuments in Bath, just sufficient survives to allow a tolerably reliable reconstruction to be attempted (72).

By any standards a tholos of this size and elaboration is an unusual type of building to find in the western provinces but then Bath is an unusual sanctuary. While the building's existence cannot be doubted its exact location remains very uncertain. The most likely possibility is that it stood within the precinct delimited by the massive foundations. If so, it was probably sited on the same axis as the temple of Sulis Minerva whose proportions it so exactly mirrored (73).

One further point is worth speculating on. The tholos is stylistically of Hadrianic date. Could it be that it was built at the instigation of the emperor when he visited Britain in AD 122? A building of this type, inspired by Hellenistic architecture, would not have been out of place as the gift of a man so immersed in Greek culture.

The eastern and northern limits of the tholos precinct are entirely unknown. Our interpretation, assuming the structure to be square, is entirely speculative but it has the advantage of allowing the east side of the precinct to align approximately with the east end of the bathing establishment. Beyond this eastern limit several trial trenches,

73 *The possible location of the tholos.*

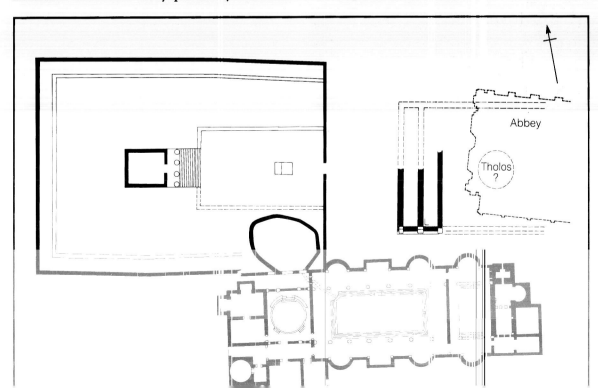

between the abbey and York Street, have revealed a thick and multi-phased deposit of compacted gravel suggesting the existence of an extensive open area. Its limits are yet to be defined. During an excavation undertaken immediately south of the abbey in 1993 for the construction of the Abbey Heritage Vaults, remains of Roman buildings were discovered constructed across the gravel spread in the late third century. The presence of stone moulds used in the manufacture of pewter vessels suggests that the building may have served as a shop or workshop representing the encroachment of commercial buildings on a previously open public space.

The Westgate Street monument

The fragments described here rather grandly as 'the Westgate Street monument' are more elusive of interpretation. All that now remain are four fragments of sculptured cornice from a gigantic monument, which came to light in 1869 during the rebuilding of the Pump Room Hotel; needless to say, it was James Irvine who was responsible for their preservation. The largest fragment is part of an elaborately sculptured cornice in the centre of which is set a larger-than-life-sized face of apparently human form, serving as a gargoyle to

74 *The cornice of a massive monumental building found in Westgate Street. It bears human heads, which act as gargoyles, carved at intervals between formal fleur-de-lis type motifs. Height 46.5cm (18¼in).*

disperse the rain-water accumulating in a gutter cut into the upper surface (**74**). The other, smaller, pieces probably belonged to the same entablature. Compared with the cornice of the temple, this monument must have been about twice as large. One possibility is that it may have been part of a theatre but there is no proof of this. However, in a sanctuary as important as Aquae Sulis there is most likely to have been a theatre for religious performances. No doubt it will one day be located. The most likely place to look would be just north of the temple where the land rises quite steeply.

The Hot Baths

The spring which served the main bathing establishment was the most copious source in the settlement, but there were two other subsidiary springs in the south-west corner of the enclosed area, one now serving the Hot Baths and another the Cross Bath. Both were used during the Roman period (**75, 76**).

Between 1864 and 1866 an area of land between Hot Bath Street and Beau Street was redeveloped for the new Royal United Hospital. Fortunately the building programme coincided with Irvine's residence in the town and he naturally took a considerable interest in the progress of the work, over the years producing his usual meticulous plans as well as photographs. His discoveries were of some significance. He was able to show that an early Roman building of undefined function and date was demolished and superseded by an elaborate suite of baths apparently consisting of two separate sections, a heated range and a swimming-bath. Of the heated range, the excavations exposed a large *caldarium* (?) with an apsidal bath in one end, separated by a corridor from a further *caldarium* or *tepidarium* with its floor supported on *pilae*. Evidently there had been considerable alteration in this part of the range, but the exact sequence and details are no longer clear, nor is it possible to assess the functions of the two other rooms which were linked to the corridor (**77**).

Of the plunge bath, only the corner lay within the area available for excavation, but enough

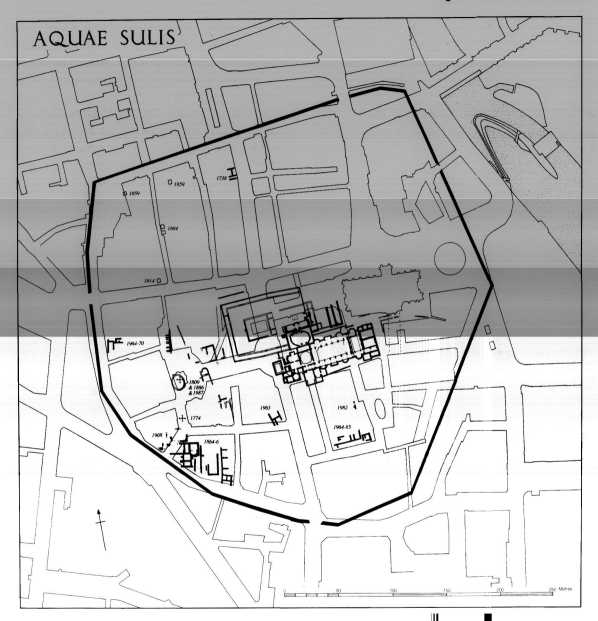

AQUAE SULIS

75 *General plan of the walled area of Roman Bath.*

survived to show that a flight of six steps descended into the lead-lined tank. In the rubble close by, the excavators found the base of a pier with attached pilasters identical in style to the piers in the main baths. The bath and presumably the establishment to which it belonged was clearly of some quality and importance. In fact there can

It is probable that the establishment was in some way dedicated to a deity or deities, but of the religious aspects of the building we are ignorant except for several altars from the neighbourhood. Two were recovered when the

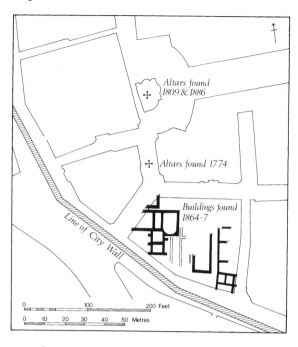

76 *The south-west corner of the town.*

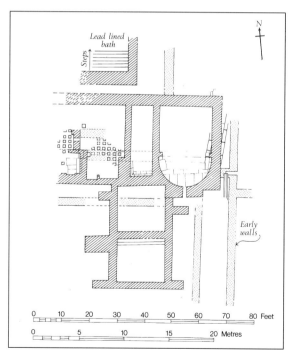

77 *Plan of the Roman Hot Baths redrawn after J.T. Irvine.*

Diana. Another altar was found nearby in 1825 during building work connected with the United Hospital. The deity for whom it was set up is unknown but the suppliant is recorded as 'son of Novantius' who erected the altar on behalf of himself and his family. Together the three inscriptions imply that the Roman Hot Bath spring possessed strong religious connections – a point further emphasized by a large number of coins found in the spring in the eighteenth century.

The Cross Bath

The spring now occupied by the Cross Bath was also used in the Roman period, but there is no evidence of elaborate building. The first Roman discovery was made in 1809 when the cistern was cleared out: from a depth of 4m (13ft), workmen recovered an altar dedicated to Sulis Minerva and the Divine Household of the Emperor by a soldier, Gaius Curiatius Saturninus. An even more interesting find was made in 1885 while Davis was having the cistern cleared again. This time, from a depth of 6m (20ft), a carved block was brought up, depicting scenes from the Aesculapius legend, a very appropriate fitting for a curative spring since Aesculapius was a deity associated with healing. At the same time, an uninscribed altar and the 'walls of the Roman well' were found, but there is a tantalizing lack of further detail.

In 1987 limited explorations in and around the Cross Bath established that the spring had been contained within a large oval walled enclosure, 12 by 10m (39 by 33ft), the wall surviving to 2m (6½ft) in height, suggesting that it may have been simply an open pool designed for viewing and perhaps for worship. A sluice at the south side would have allowed water to flow towards the Hot Baths.

Roman building in Abbeygate Street

In contrast to the hasty and ill-recorded discoveries of the eighteenth and nineteenth centuries, it has been possible to carry out several small excavations within the town at a reasonably leisurely pace, in an attempt to trace the occupation of selected areas from the time the site was first inhabited until the construction of cellars during the eighteenth century. One of these sites lay on the north side of Abbeygate Street, beneath two houses, Nos. 4 and 5, which had been demolished down to their cellar walls, the demolition rubble fortunately being removed. Although the upstanding walls hindered excavation, it was possible to examine a large part of the site throughout the winter of 1964–5 and again in 1971. A further opportunity came in the winter of 1984–5 when buildings on the corner of Abbeygate Street and Swallow Street were demolished prior to the redevelopment of the entire block. In this piecemeal fashion it has been possible to build up a detailed picture of the development of this part of the town (**78**).

At the beginning of the Roman period and throughout the first and second centuries the site was covered with a layer of black organic mud a little over 30cm (12in) thick. A certain amount of rubbish accumulated but there appears to have been little attempt at consolidation or building until the beginning of the third century, when tips of rubble were trampled down to form a

hard standing and at least one wall was built. Evidence of leadworking in the form of lead off-cuts and ceramic tuyères (nozzles through which air is blasted) were found at this period. It was not until the late third century that any large-scale construction work was carried out, but then a fairly substantial masonry house, built of neatly coursed lias limestone masonry, was put up. Three of its rooms, floored simply with gravel and mortar, projected into the area excavated, but there was no evidence of particular comfort or elegance. At this stage the building appears to have been composed of a simple range of rooms with an open area and a gutter on the north side and possibly a corridor on the south and east. The area to the north of the building had been levelled up, probably at an earlier date, with a thick layer of concrete, though for what purpose remains unclear.

Later, during the fourth century, a number of alterations were carried out. One of the rooms was

78 *Roman buildings in Abbeygate Street.*

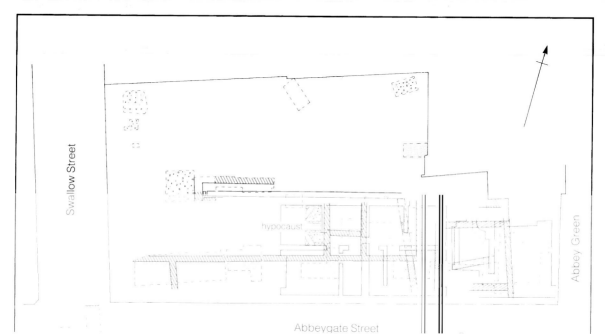

provided with central heating by means of a channelled hypocaust, and another room was for some reason divided into two. The walls were painted in green, red and white, with red predominating: sometimes areas of red paint were enlivened with frame lines painted as white bands 3mm (⅒in) thick and a few fragments of ochre paint splashed with red show that one of the rooms had been painted to represent inlaid marble. Clearly, by this stage, if not before, the building was fitted out in some style. Part of a separate house with a mortar floor and painted walls was found to the east. It too underwent modification at a later date and was partially rebuilt.

Late in the fourth century the houses collapsed. First the roof of blue pennant slabs slid off on to the mortar-floored yard to the south, taking with it the ridge blocks. No attempt was made to salvage usable building stone; instead the shell of the building was left standing, the plaster rendering gradually flaking off the walls and eventually the walls themselves falling in, or being deliberately levelled. The western part of the site now reverted to an open area over which a thick black turf-line accumulated while a completely new building was erected over the eastern part, aligned askew to the third-century building. When the destruction took place cannot be precisely defined, but as the original alterations did not take place until during the fourth century it is unlikely that the building was abandoned much before the early years of the fifth. This makes the building which followed it very late indeed, probably sub-Roman. If it was not actually built after AD 410, it must surely have continued in use for some considerable time afterwards, for inside a sequence of occupation levels was discovered. First a small oven was built in a hole cut into the mortar floor, and only after a thick layer of ash had accumulated around it was a new floor of clay laid. How long all this lasted is completely unknown, but before the building was finally abandoned the severed head of a young woman was flung into the oven – suggesting perhaps a decline in civilized standards of living. There can be very little doubt, therefore, that the occupation

of this site continued long after the official abandonment of the British province in AD 410. We may well be looking at Bath during the uneasy period at the end of the fifth century.

Citizen House

A small plot of derelict land in the western part of the walled area was eagerly seized upon during the first campaign of excavations and in 1964 several trial trenches were dug showing just how prolific of Roman structures the site was (**79**). In consequence when, in 1970, the intention to put up a new building on the site was announced, a more extended programme of work was put in hand.

The sequence of occupation spanned the Roman period beginning with timber-built houses in the late first century but quickly developing with masonry houses in the early second century. In both phases the buildings had plastered walls which were attractively painted, while the later masonry building could boast glazed windows. In the second half of the second century the site was cleared and a new masonry building erected. Its outer walls were masonry but the internal partitions were of plastered timber studwork based on dwarf masonry sills. The building was extended and refloored on several occasions throughout the third and fourth centuries during which time it seems to have served as a workshop of some kind. At one stage two small bowl furnaces were in use for forging iron using Somerset coal as the fuel. Eventually in the latter part of the fourth century the building was abandoned and fell into disrepair, a thick layer of soil developing above it.

Although the main sequence could be worked out in some detail the plan recovered was very scrappy because this area had become back gardens in Saxon and medieval times and was densely pocked with cesspits and rubbish-pits of the ninth to thirteenth centuries. After so much pit-digging activity comparatively little of the Roman stratigraphy was left intact!

Nos 9–13 Bath Street

The redevelopment of the properties immediately to the west of the temple forecourt in 1986 allowed

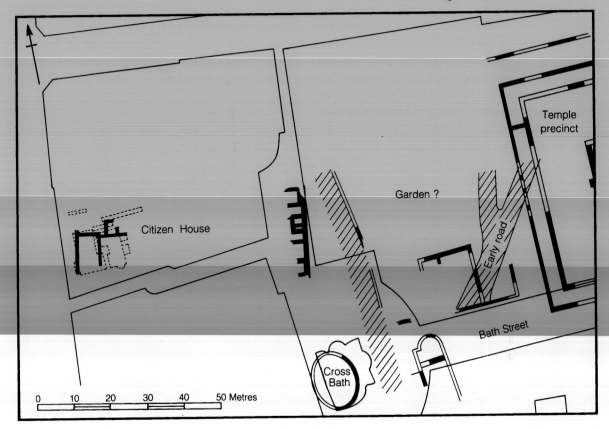

79 *Roman buildings on the site of Citizen House.*

a large area of the Roman settlement to be examined, but the extent of previous disturbance and the speed of the new development meant that only the broad picture could be rescued.

The most interesting feature was a road some 4m (13ft) wide which ran diagonally across the site south-west to north-east and can be dated to the decade immediately following the invasion of AD 43, the early date suggesting that it may have been of military origin. When the temple was laid out in the 60s and 70s the precinct impinged upon the line so the road had to be diverted around the north-western corner. Even so the road system was short-lived. By the mid-second century it had gone out of use and a masonry building was erected across its line. Much of the area to the

north–south street, to the west of which a substantial building was constructed in the fourth century. Too little of the building survived to be sure of its function but the small rooms into which it was divided are reminiscent of the cubicles of an inn (*mansio*). Whether the structure was part of that discovered on the site of Citizen House in 1964–70 remains unclear.

The excavation identified the apse of another large building of fourth-century date running under Bath Street. Further work in the cellar of nos. 7 and 7a on the south side of Bath Street showed that the building ran beneath the line of the present street. The apse is suggestive that it may have been part of yet another bathing establishment.

Beau Street Swimming-Baths

the 1980s to renovate the area. Although nothing has yet come of them, the proposed developments provided an opportunity for some limited archaeological investigation. Work has not yet been completed but a succession of structures was noted beginning with a substantial stone-capped drain running north-east to south-west. The drain trench was subsequently recut as a ditch and not refilled until the middle of the second century after which a succession of buildings occupied the site aligned north–south and east–west. The mid-second-century replanning, which involved the abandonment of the earlier alignment, is matched at the site of 9–13 Bath Street and may indicate a major redevelopment of Bath at this time.

Nos 30–31 Stall Street

In 1964–5 two shops in Stall Street were demolished and rebuilt as part of the same efficiently organized operation. Apart from a single trial trench cut in a cellar before the rebuilding began, archaeological work had to be restricted to recording and salvaging while the new building was being erected: the results are accordingly less detailed than they would have been had the work progressed more slowly under strict archaeological control. Nevertheless, the main sequence of occupation was determined (**80**). At a depth of 4m (13ft) below street level the original black organic turf-line was found overlaid by a series of floors belonging to timber-framed Roman buildings, but no details of their plans could be recovered. The destruction of one of the buildings was marked by a thick layer of fine, brown, sandy clay interspersed with paper-thin patches of paint, which is all that now remains of a painted wattle and daub wall after it had collapsed and its timber framework had rotted. From the stratified pottery recovered from these levels it seems that the buildings date from the late first or early second century.

Late in the second century or early in the third the site was levelled with rubble and a substantial Roman masonry building was erected, of which only a small part lay within the development

80 *Roman building beneath 30–31 Stall Street.*

area. No indication of its size and function has yet been discovered but its central position and massive construction suggest that it was a building of some importance.

Abbey Green

Not all archaeological finds in Bath in recent years have been made as the result of planned archaeological excavation. A good example of a

81 *Roman mosaic found beneath the Crystal Palace public house in Abbey Green.*

chance find was made when the proprietor of the Crystal Palace public house was digging to modify one of his cellars and almost immediately came upon a fragment of a fine mosaic pavement (**81**). Only part was exposed but the rest is probably well preserved beneath the yard of the pub. Stylistically the floor would appear to be of late second-century date. It had been laid in a room added to an earlier building. Later the mosaic was covered by a mortar floor containing pottery of the third or fourth century. A small trial trench dug in the cellar of the house immediately to the north showed that the house with the mosaic was preceded by a thick deposit of occupation and building debris over a metre thick, indicating intense activity in this part of the town.

Other Roman buildings from the centre of the settlement

In addition to the more important sites recorded above, a number of other fragments of buildings have come to light since the beginning of the eighteenth century, most of them ill-recorded. But as they provide some idea of the structure and elaboration of the settlement, a brief description of the more substantial remains must be given.

Irvine's rescue work on the site of the United Hospital has already been mentioned in relation to the Roman bathing establishment which he discovered, but the site was a large one and over much of the eastern area a substantial part of what appears to be a town house was recovered (see **76**). Altogether, about seven rooms were exposed, one of which contained a pillared hypocaust supporting a mosaic 3.2m (10ft) square depicting a central rosette enclosed within a semi-geometric border (**82**). Irvine believed that a 3m (10ft) wide road ran along the west side of the building towards the temple precinct.

Part of another large house was found in 1738 while the south-east part of the Mineral Water Hospital was being built. Fortunately, the architect

82 *Drawing of a mosaic found on the site of the Royal United Hospital.*

linked by through-vents to another heated room next door. Close by were two mosaics. One belonged to a corridor 1.8m (6ft) wide, the other, 5.5m (18ft) across, was evidently from an important room: it was a fine mosaic decorated with intertwined circles. In the north wall a wide doorway, reached by two steps, led up to another room or courtyard paved with slabs. Clearly the house to which these fragments belonged was of some elaboration.

Another tessellated floor was found nearby when further building work was carried out in 1859. All that now survives is a fragment of blue and white Greek key design exposed in the basement of the hospital, but the contemporary records suggest the existence of a substantial house with floors of concrete and hypocausts. It was from this site that part of a marble inscription, mentioning Tiberius Claudius Sollemnis, was found.

Some way to the south, in Bridewell Lane, yet

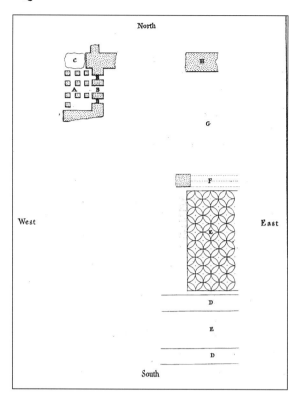

83 *The first Roman building to be recorded in detail was a house exposed early in the eighteenth century by the architect John Wood the elder during the building of the Mineral Water Hospital. Wood's plan is reproduced here.*

84 *Mosaic exposed in Bridewell Lane; now destroyed.*

85 *Mosaic from the Bluecoat School now preserved in the Roman Baths Museum.*

panels containing rosettes (**84**) rather similar to the rosette in the centre of Irvine's mosaic below the United Hospital. Yet another mosaic was found on the corner of Bridewell Lane and Westgate Street in 1814. The Reverend Scarth says, 'it was not of superior elegance in design or workmanship' and it appears that it was soon broken up. A much finer floor was found in the north-east corner of the settlement when alterations were made to the Bluecoat School in 1859. It depicts a freely drawn scene of fabulous sea-beasts in red, blue and brown against a plain white background (**85**). The fragment was lifted and is now exhibited in the Roman Baths Museum. Finally, another semi-geometric mosaic was found south of the Abbeygate Street building when Weymouth House School was being reconstructed in 1897. This, too, has been lifted and is now on view in the museum.

There are, of course, large numbers of other objects and fragmentary structures from the town but these are either of little general significance or are badly recorded and located. The above summary does, however, show that the central part of the settlement possessed buildings of some quality. At least eleven are known and there must be others, but whether they were private houses, guest-houses or the houses of the staff of the temple and baths we are unlikely ever to know.

The town 'defences'

Having discussed the buildings within the nucleus of the Roman settlement, it is necessary to turn to the difficult problem of the town defences. There is, of course, no doubt that the town was enclosed within a city wall from medieval times until the eighteenth century (see **75**), when the wall began to be removed to make way for the expanding town. The question is: When was the wall built? The accounts of early excavations across the line give little idea. In 1795, Governor Pownall records 'a Roman wall 15 feet [4.6m] thick built of a rubble and concrete core faced with large stone blocks' exposed at the south end of Old Bond Street. In 1803 building work close to the Northgate uncovered a wall of massive blocks including much reused Roman architectural material, and later still, in 1865, Irvine recorded an exposure of the south wall 1.7m thick (5½ft), opposite the end of Hot Bath Street. None of these discoveries, however, gives any indication of the initial construction date of the defences.

One of the first tasks to confront the newly formed Bath Excavation Committee in 1963 was the excavation of an area in Upper Borough Walls about to be redeveloped by Messrs Harveys Ltd. The site, which lay along the back of the north wall, provided an admirable opportunity for excavation geared to examine the problems of the northern defences of the town.

Without waiting for the demolition of the existing building, occupied by the wine merchants Cater, Stoffel and Fortts, excavation began amid the well-stocked wine vaults. Immediately it became apparent that the city wall lay somewhere to the north of the cellars beneath the building, but fortunately it was found that the road, Upper Borough Walls, was built over cellars which communicated directly with the basements of the buildings on both sides. Therefore by working north from Cater, Stoffel and Fortts and south from the buildings on the opposite side of the road, it was possible to obtain an almost complete section through the defensive works (**86**).

Several interesting facts emerged. To begin with, it appears that the north side of the town was defended by a rampart of gravel and clay, more than 2m (6½ft) high and 9.1m (30ft) wide, presumably fronted by a ditch or ditches. A careful examination of material from within the structure of the bank showed that the latest pottery dated to the later years of the second century, while from the layers of occupation rubbish which had accumulated later over the tail of the rampart quantities of third- and fourth-century pottery were recovered. Although the evidence is far from conclusive, it tends to suggest that the

86 *Sections through the city defences at Upper Borough Walls.*

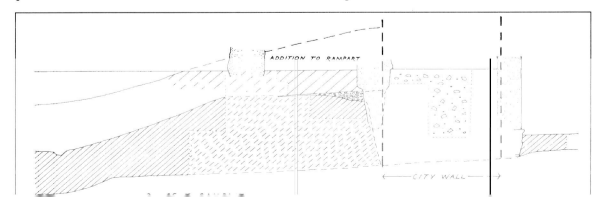

ADDITION TO RAMPART

← CITY WALL →

rampart should be dated broadly to the late second or early third century.

Attention then switched to the north side of the road where, in two small and extremely awkwardly placed trenches in the less congenial cellars of the Accident Prevention Office, a mass of rubble representing the destroyed and robbed remains of the town wall was sectioned, together with part of its rubble and clay footing dug through early Roman levels. Clearly the point of greatest interest was at the junction between the Roman rampart and the wall but, as the drawing (see **86**) shows, the crucial levels had been thoroughly destroyed by the nineteenth-century spine wall which supported the modern road. Even so, all was not lost, for the trench exposed the top of the early rampart, upon which a thin layer of turf had begun to accumulate, sealed by a thick mass of fresh stone chippings. Above this, masses of clay had been thrown down to heighten the rampart. A *possible* explanation of these observations is that the layer of chippings was deposited when the town wall was inserted into the front of the rampart. Since only a very thin turf-line had formed, the deposition of the chippings cannot have taken place very long after the original construction of the rampart. If therefore the chippings belong to the construction of a wall, the wall is likely to be third century or later. Everything hangs on the 'if'. In favour of this interpretation it may be said that late second-century ramparts with third-century walls inserted tend to be a frequently repeated pattern elsewhere in Roman Britain. Bath would seem to echo the norm.

Another opportunity to examine the northern defences came in 1980 when the entire insula between Upper Borough Walls and New Bond Street came up for development. Trial trenching showed that the wall had been fronted by a berm (area of level ground) before the edge of a wide flat-bottomed ditch was encountered. This kind of arrangement is quite common among fourth-century defensive circuits and might suggest that the walls of Bath are late Roman in origin.

The question raised by the northern defences clearly demanded the digging of more rampart sections elsewhere around the town, but unfortunately there is at present not a single square metre of available land in the right position. Eighteenth-century builders have covered the defences either with roads or with buildings of merit, whose well-being is closely guarded by the preservationists. Nevertheless, a considerable section of the outer face of the city wall still survives along the southeast side of the town and an examination of the structure at several points along its line, particularly after the clearance of accumulated rubbish from in front of it, strongly suggests that the work is Roman to a considerable height (**87**). The neat coursing and the evenness of size of the blocks give the wall a striking resemblance to good Roman

87 *The outer face of the city wall, seen here behind the Fernley Hotel, is built of neat coursed masonry typical of Roman work, but no positive dating evidence has been found to show that the wall is Roman. (Scale in feet.)*

work, but again, until excavation is possible through the layers behind the wall, final answers will not be forthcoming. We are forced, therefore, to the rather unsatisfactory conclusion that, while all the existing evidence points to a Roman origin for the town wall at Bath, proof is still lacking. Nor is it necessary for us to suppose that a Roman wall, if it existed, was exactly followed by the later medieval city wall. Indeed a series of trenches cut at Seven Dials Car Park in 1990 and 1991 failed to identify any defensive Roman structure. The problem therefore remains. If, however, we allow that a Roman wall was built to enclose the principal buildings of the sanctuary, two possible interpretations present themselves: either the wall was defensive and built at a time when other cities in Britain were looking to their own protection, or it was constructed to delineate the sanctuary and was therefore a temenos boundary. The two possibilities are not necessarily exclusive.

The settlement beyond the walls

The wall now encloses an area of a little under 10ha (25 acres), about a quarter the size of the normal Romano-British cantonal capital. Whatever may be thought of the status of the walled area of Roman Bath it is hardly surprising that the occupied area extended beyond the wall and straggled along the road leading north from the Northgate, in the form of what appears to be a ribbon development. Further areas of occupation have been found across the river at Bathwick.

Our knowledge of the extra-mural settlement is very patchy, but quantities of occupation material of the second century have been recovered from time to time in the Walcot area, Old Orchard Lane, Guinea Lane and the Paragon, leaving little doubt that these areas were intensively inhabited. Occasionally fragments of buildings have turned up. In 1902, just north of Old Orchard Lane on the east side of Walcot Street, five pier bases, each 1.7m (5½ft) apart, were seen, together with what

1854–5 suggest the site of yet another building. Other Roman structures include a drain and area of pavement found when a sewer was being laid close to the Northgate, 12m (39ft) south of St Michael's Church in 1913.

Not far from the church, to the east, the building of the Beaufort (now Bath Hilton) Hotel and multi-storey car park in 1971 exposed a Roman pit dug down into the impermeable blue lias clay. The contents had remained waterlogged since Roman times and preserved a magnificent collection of Roman shoes, together with leather offcuts and small iron tools, suggestive of the existence nearby of a cobbler's shop. The pottery from the pit is of late second-century date. Together with the ironworking debris at Citizen House, the pewter moulds south of the abbey and the traces of a plumber's workshop at Abbeygate Street a picture of the artisans of Roman Bath is beginning to emerge.

A series of trial excavations, carried out at various times between 1987 and 1991 on development sites between London Road and the River Avon just south of Cleveland Bridge, has produced evidence of dense occupation which seems to have developed around the ford just downstream from the present bridge. Occupation seems to have spanned the Roman period and by the second and third century comprised densely packed buildings with narrow lanes between. As the map (88) shows, a number of Roman roads appear to converge on the ford which may well have been the main river-crossing, at least in the early Roman period. It is hardly surprising that dense settlement should have developed around the ford.

From this perspective one might argue that Bath had two foci – the ford near Cleveland Bridge and the springs on lower land to the south in the bend of the river. Each developed in its own way with ribbon development along the road between them.

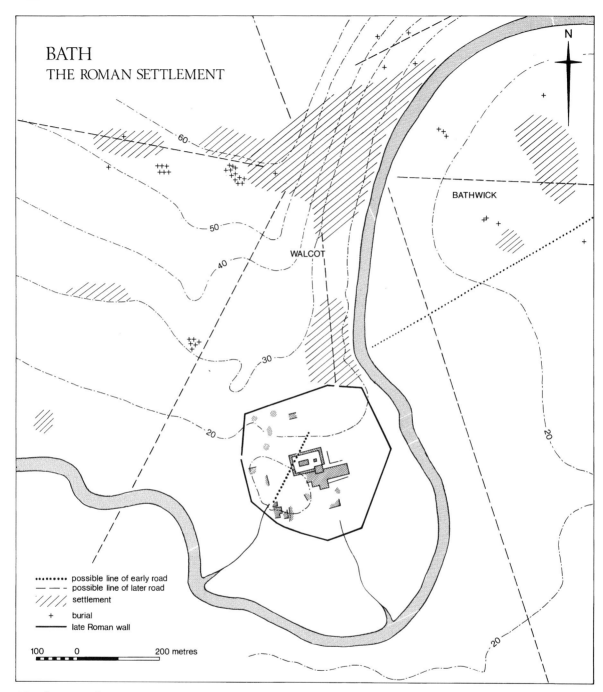

88 *The extent of the Roman settlement at Aquae Sulis.*

than it provides answers: Bath is a peculiar settlement, in size much smaller than typical Roman market towns, in elaboration much greater. Its position, at the crossing point of the Fosseway and the River Avon, would have endowed it with

a certain military significance in the middle years of the first century when, for a short time, the Fosse formed part of the frontier defences of the newly won province. The road would have been provided with a chain of forts placed at strategic intervals. One of these may well have occupied the gravel terrace on the Bathwick side of the river where early samian pottery of pre-Flavian (before AD 69) date has been found. A fort in this position would have been admirably situated to guard the strategic river-crossing upon which all the major roads appear to converge (see **88**). Another possible fort site is the Queen's Square area where some cremation burials were found. No physical trace of military structure has yet been found at either site but the early military tombstones are additional evidence of the fort's existence and it can only be a matter of time before its position is located. The only structure which might be considered to be of military origin is the early road running diagonally across the Bath Street site pre-dating the construction of the temple precinct.

The springs gushing out of the ground below the 30m (100ft) terrace seem to have been developed at an early stage, during the latter half of the first century. The Great Baths were built, the first stage of the temple was probably laid out, together perhaps with the adjacent court, and there must have been many subsidiary buildings such as hotels and rest-houses; in fact all the facilities of a successful spa. That the place was a success is shown by the inscriptions left by visitors, who by the beginning of the second century were travelling long distances to Bath. At this stage it seems that apart from the principal buildings much of the later walled area was underdeveloped land, probably without a systematically laid out street grid – in fact little more than a series of buildings and precincts centred on the springs and linked perhaps by pathways. The main settlement area of the second century seems to have remained on the relatively level, well-drained gravel to the north along the line of the Fosseway towards the Cleveland Bridge ford and across the river in the area of Bathwick.

In the mid-second century the public buildings were probably enclosed first with a rampart and ditch and later, in the fourth century, with a

on previously open ground, packed tightly between existing buildings. It may be that the northern settlement area was gradually abandoned as people migrated into the walled area, and Roman Bath began to take on the appearance of a more typical Romano-British town (**colour plate 12**). In the fourth century buildings were actually impinging on the old temple precincts.

Two reasons have been mentioned for the early growth of the settlement: the military significance of the river-crossing and the tourist value of the hot springs. Once it had begun to develop, the economic significance of the site would soon have become apparent. Bath was conveniently sited on a road junction where roads from London, Poole Harbour and Sea Mills (a port close to the mouth of the Avon), converged on the Fosseway, which linked the West Country and the Midlands. It also lay in the centre of a rich production area for corn, wool, stone and pewter. Whatever its origins, it cannot have failed to have developed as an important market centre, particularly in the fourth century, by which time the surrounding countryside was densely packed with the villa estates of rich landowners – more than twenty-eight villas are known within a 24km (15 mile) radius of the town. There is nothing unusual in a religious centre being associated with marketing activities – the combination occurs frequently in the Roman world. Indeed, it is not at all unlike the fairs of medieval England, which were always associated with the celebration of saints' days.

One remaining problem is the status of Bath. Aquae Sulis is listed, along with Winchester, as one of the towns in the administrative territory of the Belgae. While there can be no doubt that Winchester was the principal centre, a strong probability remains that Bath served as a seat of regional government for the western part of the territory – it is, after all, 80km (50 miles) from Winchester and a good 48km (39 miles) from the nearest large towns. No area of this size and eco-

6

The people of Roman Bath

Over the years casual excavations in Bath have yielded an amazing haul of Roman inscriptions of various kinds: more than forty are now known and there must be many more still to be found. Altogether they provide a unique insight into the composition of the community, mentioning no less than 33 different people. Not all sections of the community are represented, however, for the poorer people could hardly afford to erect altars to the gods, nor could their families find the money to pay for tombstones for them when they died; but as the survey will show, artisans and retired soldiers were certainly wealthy enough to record themselves for posterity, along with the more high-ranking members of the community. To this group of inscriptions we should add the pewter curses found in the sacred spring. Together they list scores of individuals by name, many of whom would have come from the poorer classes.

Inhabitants and visitors

To begin with the residents of social distinction, we know of only one priest from the Temple of Sulis, Gaius Calpurnius Receptus, who died at the age of 75 and was buried in what is now Sydney Gardens. His tombstone, a simple affair carved piously in the form of an altar, was put up by his wife, Calpurnia Trifosa, who had originally been his slave, but to whom he had at some stage granted freedom – presumably before the marriage. The freeing of slaves is recorded a second time in Bath on two altars found within the

temple precinct, erected for the same man, Marcus Aufidius Maximus, a retired centurion of the Sixth Legion Victrix, one by Aufidius Eutuches, the other by Marcus Aufidius Lemnus. Both men are referred to as 'his freedman', suggesting perhaps an act of thanks for the master by two of his newly freed slaves.

Another of the temple employees was Lucius Marcius Memor, whose inscribed statue base has already been mentioned (see **26**). As a *haruspex* he would have been a member of an élite class of augurs who officiated in the principal temples of the empire, foretelling the future through their closely guarded knowledge of omens. One wonders whether he would have been a resident in Bath, working full-time in the temple, or simply a visitor passing through. Two other dignitaries connected with the temple have already been referred to: Claudius Ligur and Gaius Protacius, who were responsible for the restoration and repainting of a monument or building belonging to the temple. Both were probably public-minded citizens willing to show their devotion to the gods, and incidentally to their fellows, by making a donation in aid of good works.

Bath must have had something of a cosmopolitan air about it in the Roman period, not unlike the town today at the height of the holiday season. There were the retired soldiers living in and around the town, soldiers on leave visiting the spring, and a constant stream of tourists from Britain and abroad, all drawn to the spa by stories of the curative properties of the waters. Some

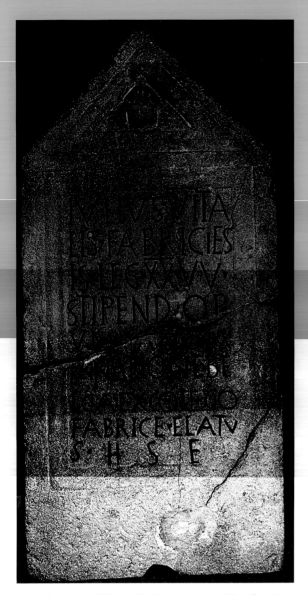

89 *Tombstone of Julius Vitalis, armourer of the Twentieth Legion, erected by members of the craft guild to which he belonged. Height 1.85m (6ft).*

the title of the legion, a fact which suggests that the tombs were erected at an early date in the first century, before the legion had won the honours, at which time the two soldiers may well have been on active service. Whatever may have been the position of these three, other soldiers recorded from the town were visitors or retired veterans choosing the enervating atmosphere of Bath in which to spend their declining years. Some of the soldiers died at an unnaturally early age, people such as Julius Vitalis (**89**), an armourer of the Twentieth Legion recruited in Gallia Belgica, who died after only nine years' service, aged 29; and Gaius Murrius Modestus, of the Second Adiutrix Legion, from Forum Julii, in southern France, who died aged 25. They must have been ailing from disease or wounds when they visited Bath, never to return to their legions. Vitalis belonged to a craft guild, equivalent now to a Friendly Society. When he died his colleagues paid for his cremation and tombstone, carefully recording on it, 'with funeral at the cost of the Guild of Armourers'. Even a young soldier could be assured of a decent burial if he belonged to a guild.

Other soldiers settled in Bath after demobilization (**90**). Marcus Aufidius Maximus, the centurion of the Sixth Legion, has already been mentioned in relation to the slaves he freed. By this time he was probably a prosperous local figure living in comfortable retirement. Another soldier, unnamed, probably settled in the north suburbs of the town, where he lost his bronze diploma issued to all soldiers on their retirement. He had served in a cavalry regiment, the *ala I Gallorum Proculeiana*, early in the second century and like all time-expired veterans was granted the right of citizenship after twenty-five years' service. As a man in his mid-forties, he and possibly his family chose Bath as a congenial town in which to begin his new life, perhaps as a craftsman, a farmer or a merchant. There must have

of the soldiers, like the cavalryman Lucius Vitellius Tancinus, a Spaniard from Caurium serving with the *ala Vettonum*, who died at the age of 46 after twenty-six years of service, may possibly have been stationed at the supposed fort at

90 *Tombstone of a cavalry man.*

still on active service with his legion stationed at Caerleon just across the Bristol Channel? We know of him because of the altar he set up at the Cross Bath spring to Sulis Minerva and to the deities of the emperors, either in repayment for a request which the goddess had answered, or in anticipation of a satisfactory response.

Less certainty attaches to the standing of the centurion Gaius Severius Emeritus, who dedicated an altar (**91**) recording his act of piety in cleansing afresh 'this holy spot wrecked by insolent hands'. He styles himself 'centurion in charge of this region', implying that he may have been a military administrator, perhaps responsible for a nearby imperial estate. The Roman settlement at Combe Down, near Bath, has produced an inscription recording a *principia* which is thought to refer to the headquarters of local procuratorial administration, and a lead seal found on the same site, stamped *p(rovinciae) Br(itanniae) S(uperioris)* shows that official parcels were passing through. It may be that Emeritus ran the establishment for a while. It is interesting to question whose 'insolent hands' wrecked the holy place with which Emeritus was concerned. Could it perhaps have been the Christians who, in the new-found power of the official recognition afforded to them in the early fourth century, would have found much to react against in the great pagan centre of Bath? There must have been many, like Emeritus, ready to restore the old pagan order when the wave of iconoclasm had passed.

Bath lay at the centre of a rich stone-producing area, and its fine-grained cream-coloured oolitic limestone soon became well known and widely used throughout the province. We know of two masons who visited the spa: Priscus, son of Toutius (**92**) and Sulinus, son of Brucetius (**93**), both recorded on inscribed dedicatory altars.

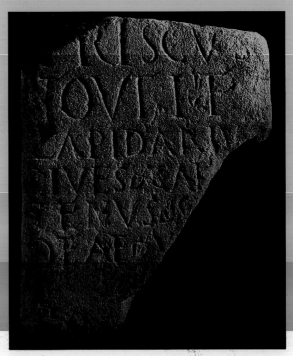

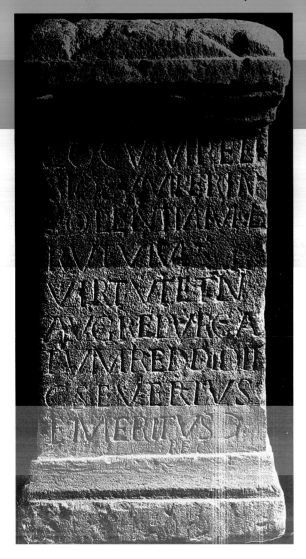

92 *Priscus, son of Toutius, a stonemason from Chartres, erected this for the goddess Sulis. Height 53cm (21in).*

The Priscus inscription was found close to the baths and is dedicated to Sulis, while the offering of Sulinus, which may also have come from the main temple, was dedicated to a collection of local deities, the Suleviae. Priscus originated from the tribe of the Carnutes centred on modern Chartres. As a *lapidarius* (stoneworker) he must have taken a professional interest in the local stone quarries, but even if he was on a business trip he would presumably have indulged in the pleasures that Bath had to offer. Sulinus, who styles himself a sculptor, poses more interesting problems because the same man is recorded on an altar, again dedicated to the Suleviae, discovered at Cirencester. 45km (28 miles) north of Bath. The inscription was found at Ashcroft towards the west side of the Roman town in 1899, together with eight other sculptured stones, all in a well-preserved fresh condition. Two of

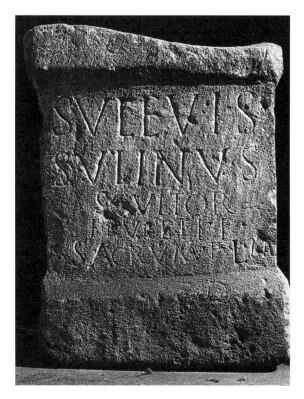

93 *Altar to the Suleviae, erected by the sculptor Sulinus who may have lived and worked in Cirencester. Height 59cm (23in).*

the fourth was a base for a similar piece. The other objects included the head of a female, an inscribed altar and two pieces of columns. Exactly how this collection should be interpreted is uncertain. It may be the remains of a shrine or temple, but the fresh nature of the individual carvings is certainly suggestive of a mason's working yard, as the original excavator thought. If so, it may be the workshop of Sulinus. Did he perhaps visit Bath to buy stone from the local quarries? Some of the pieces from the Cirencester yard are carved from Bath stone, but this of course proves nothing. The facts as we know them are full of fascinating possibilities but they leave the situation wide open.

One other stoneworker should be mentioned: the unnamed craftsman who engraved the superb collection of gemstones found within the culvert leading from the spring reservoir. A recent study of the individual intaglios leaves little doubt that all 33 gems were engraved by the same school of craftsmen or even perhaps the same man. Someone put them in a bag and flung it into the spring as an offering to the deity. Was it the engraver himself dedicating a sample of his work or did someone else buy them from him? If it was the craftsman, did he work in Bath, gearing his output to the tourist industry, or was he a visitor? These are questions to which we will never know the answers.

The stonemason Priscus from Chartres is a reminder of the great attraction that the spa must have provided. People would have flocked to the town, some from other parts of the Roman world. Some erected altars to the gods for their safe journey or their recovery or for some other service, while those less favoured by the gods died, only to be commemorated by their tombstones. Several visitors have already been mentioned, but we know of others. Rusonia Aventina, a middle-aged lady of the Mediomatrici, a tribe centred on Metz, died in Bath at the age of 58. She was buried in the cemetery to the north of the town by her heir, Lucius Ulpius Sestius. Was he perhaps a relation who had escorted her from home? Did he come across especially for the funeral? Or was he someone the lady had met in Britain? Again, intriguing but unanswerable questions.

Another foreigner, Peregrinus son of Secundus, a Treveran in origin from the area around modern Trier (**94**), offered an altar to his two favourite deities, Loucetius Mars and Nemetona. This particular inscription was one of the group found in 1753 at the 'holy place' at the lower end of Stall Street possibly adjacent to the precinct of the Temple of Sulis Minerva. Most of these were dedicated to gods other than Sulis Minerva, suggesting a separate shrine, a place where travellers could thank their own patron gods for a safe journey without risk of disrespect to the presiding deity.

It is a great pity that so little survives to enable the social round of the visitor to be reconstructed. Visits to the baths, temple and theatre would naturally have featured prominently and there must have been hotels (*mansiones*) for the comfort of travellers, but of the shops, taverns and other facilities offering amusement and distraction, we are at present ignorant. It is possible, too, that there were dormitories provided for the sick or for those who wished to spend time in solitary meditation, like the building found in the great pagan centre at Lydney on the other side of the Bristol Channel, where Nodens was worshipped. One man, the son of Novantius, had a vision which led him to set up a dedicatory inscription on behalf of himself and his family. This might have happened while he was in the town, but it could equally well be that the gods directed him to go there. There must have been many in this position roaming the precincts of the spa, the devout seeking out the magicians and the soothsayers, the sick visiting doctors and opticians. One doctor, Tiberius Junianus, lost his medicine stamp which eventually turned up 1500 years later in 1731, when a cellar was constructed near the Abbey Yard. Bath would have been a happy hunting-ground for skilled medical practitioners, quacks and charlatans alike; tourists on holiday are always easy prey.

In spite of the watchful eye of the goddess and the salubrious atmosphere, the death-rate here, as elsewhere in the empire, was high, and people died young. One tombstone, seen by Leland built into the town wall west of the Northgate, records the death of a little girl, Successa Petronia. It was put up by her parents, Vettius Romulus and Victoria Sabina, and mentions that she lived to 3 years 4 months and 9 days. Another girl, the foster-daughter of Magnius, called Mercatilla, was only 18 months old when she died. Her tombstone, found in 1809 near the Northgate, probably came from the cemetery which grew up along the Fosseway. In the same cemetery lay a young woman whose funerary inscription simply records: 'Vibia Jucunda, aged 30, lies buried here.' But not everyone died in youth: one old town councillor (decurion) from the colonia in

slab of white Italian marble, his name linked to that of Sulis, suggesting perhaps that he endowed a rich monument to the goddess. An altar put up by another of the deity's devotees, Quintus Pompeius Anicetus, was found in York Street; and finally yet another altar, erected by Sulinus son of Maturus, was dedicated to the same deity, this time at the Hot Bath spring. The survey of those who inhabited or visited the spring in the Roman period has been long, but it demonstrates how fortunate the archaeologists of Bath are to have so full a record, unparalleled in Britain outside the military north. The rows of dull-looking inscriptions which now fill the Roman Baths Museum

can very easily be turned into a complex picture of a vigorous Roman community.

The pewter curses thrown into the spring by aggrieved inhabitants of Bath have been discussed, in so far as they reflect on religious beliefs, in Chapter 3: here we must look briefly at what they have to say about the people. Altogether over a hundred different names are listed and occasionally we are given rare insights into family groups. Curse no. 618, which reminds the goddess of a vow sworn at the spring on 12 April, mentions six people: Uricalus, Docilosa his wife, Docilis and Docilina his son and daughter, and his brother Decentinus with his wife Alogiosa. It is interesting to see that the two brothers Uricalus and Decentinus have respectively a Celtic and a Latin name, suggesting that, in this case, their father did not recognize the difference as socially significant. But that there may, indeed, have been a status difference between Celtic and Latin names is hinted at by two more curses, nos. 206 and 612. No. 206 lists 11 names among the possible miscreants, 2 women: Severa and Surilla; and 9 men: Dracontius, Spectatus, Innocentius, Senicio, Candidianus, Simplicius, Belator, Austus and Carinianus. We are given no further details of them but two of the names, Belator and Surilla, are both Celtic while the rest are Latin. No. 612 gives us 11 names and some details about them: Roveta, Vitoria and Vindocunus her husband, Cunomolius and Minervina his wife; Cunitius the slave and Senovara his wife, Lavidendus the slave, Mattonius the slave, Catinius the tax collector's thief, and Methianus. Of this list only two, Vitoria and Minervina, have Latin names, the rest are Celtic. In this case it looks very much as though we are dealing with a group of lower-class individuals, among them three slaves. Comparing the two curses it is tempting to suggest that the families who preferred to continue using Celtic names may generally have been socially inferior. It is an interesting insight into Romano-Celtic society to be further examined as more curses are translated.

The summary of the epigraphic evidence given in the first part of this chapter gives some hint of the type of life followed by those who

lived in, or dependent upon, the town. A substantial part of the population must have been geared to providing for the tourist traffic: there were those who officiated and served in the temples and baths, the hoteliers and their servants, the doctors and the small traders, but the existence of a specialized tourist industry should not obscure the fact that Bath lay at the centre of a territory rich both agriculturally and in terms of the mineral deposits thereabouts. Some measure of local productivity can be gauged from the density of Roman villas in the countryside around the town, many of which, judging from their fine mosaic pavements, were the centres of profitable estates. Too little is yet known of the growth of individual villas to allow the economic development of the region to be traced in any detail, but in general terms the luxury villas seem to have reached their exalted status only by the beginning of the fourth century, a pattern which holds good for most parts of Britain. Elsewhere it is often possible to show a gradual rise in the material wealth of the villa owners reflected in the buildings themselves, starting with relatively unostentatious farmhouses in the first and second centuries and developing over the years by the gradual accretion of luxuries such as central heating, mosaic floors and baths. Superficially it would seem that by the fourth century a greater disparity existed in the countryside between the rich and the poor, the rich getting gradually richer while many of the peasants lived in poverty, becoming increasingly more dependent upon the large landowners.

The countryside

The agrarian wealth of the Bath region was probably based on a mixed economy in which cattle-rearing and sheep-farming would have played an important part alongside cereal production. It is impossible, in the present state of knowledge, to assess the nature of chronological or regional changes in the balance. Many of the plateau areas, such as Charmey Down and Bathampton Down, are covered with field systems suggestive of agricultural activity of some intensity; while the steep-sided valleys would have been ideal for sheep grazing, the valley floors providing lush grass for herds of cattle. It has been suggested that elsewhere in the country there was a major change-over to sheep-farming by the fourth century, wool becoming more profitable than grain since it was less heavily taxed. Whether this is generally true or not, and the matter is still in dispute, there is no firm evidence from any of the villas of the Bath region to throw light on the matter. The problem can only be resolved by new large-scale excavations of several villas.

The relationship between the villas and the town was close. Whatever the stature of Bath was in the early years of the occupation, there can be little reasonable doubt that by the third century it had developed an administrative and economic significance equivalent to that of the typical cantonal capital. It would have been ruled by a town council (*ordo*) composed of a hundred ex-magistrates (*decuriones*) who had attained certain property qualifications. These men would have lived in those country villas or town houses which might reasonably be expected to show some signs of wealth. Within a reasonable commuting distance of the town there are about thirty known villas of quality, while in the town traces of some eleven houses are at present recorded, most of which are likely to be private dwellings. The figures are *minimum* numbers, but they might suggest that the number of decurions living within the town was about a quarter of the total, the rest choosing to stay in their country estates. These calculations are, of course, rough and open to criticism but it might be significant that, on the much better evidence from Silchester, Sir Ian Richmond arrived at the same percentages.

Industrial activity

There were other sources of wealth in the area besides farming. The value of Bath stone has

for the leaseholders or owners of the workings. The very existence of the stone would have encouraged the growth of schools of craftsmen geared to the production of standard architectural details and blanks for altars and tomb reliefs. One blank altar was actually found at Bathwick in 1900 with guide-lines scribed on it ready for inscription. Perhaps it stood in the working yard of a local mason, waiting to be purchased by a visitor, first to be inscribed with suitable sentiments and then to be erected in the temple.

While there is no doubt about the economic importance of Bath stone, less certainty attaches to the exploitation of local coal. That it was used as a fuel in the neighbourhood is not in question, indeed we have seen that coal was probably burnt on the altar of Sulis Minerva, but whether a significant percentage of the population were engaged in mining or quarrying is at present an open question. Similar doubt attaches to the significance of pennant stone, a blue, closely laminated sandstone, which attained a widespread popularity as a roofing and flooring material. The local demand could probably have been easily met by the sporadic working of the quarries.

One of the more important industries of the Bath region was the manufacture of pewter vessels, which reached a peak in the fourth century. Pewter was essentially a cheap local substitute for silver, and when from the middle of the third century the unrest and economic crisis in the empire greatly increased the value of silver out of all proportion, the moderately wealthy, who required exotic-looking tableware, were forced to resort to the use of pewter, an alloy of tin and lead, which to some tastes was not found to be wholly unattractive. Why pewter manufacture should centre on Bath is not immediately apparent. Tin from Cornwall and lead from the Mendips could conveniently be transported along the Fosseway, it is true, but Ilchester is rather more centrally placed in an equally rich area. The answer may, of course, be

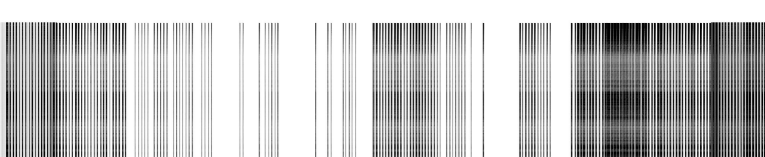

Camerton, 13km (8 miles) south of the town along the Fosseway, provides the best idea of an industrial site. Here excavation has shown the gradual growth of a ribbon development along the main road, comprised of scattered rectangular workshops 20–4m (65–79ft) long and *c.* 3m (10ft) wide, most of them provided with ovens and furnaces of a type suitable for pewter manufacture, as well as for a host of other domestic purposes. In one of the workshops two stone moulds were found, in which the metal would have been cast, one in the form of an oblong dish, the other to make a handle. From elsewhere in the settlement two other pewter plates and a handle were recovered. It would be wrong to suggest that the inhabitants of the village owed their entire livelihood to the manufacture of pewter vessels. Farming activities must have continued to play an important part in everyday life, but the growth of a specialist cottage industry would have helped the peasants to eke out a meagre existence at what must have been a very difficult period for those with little or no land of their own.

The second of the pewter production sites lies on the high land of Lansdown, about 5km (3 miles) north-west of Bath, where excavations at the beginning of the twentieth century exposed a peasant settlement of considerable extent. Quantities of fourth-century coins and pottery suggest that the greatest development came late, but there is good reason to suggest a very early origin for the settlement. Among the finds recovered is a remarkable collection of stone moulds for the production of a range of pewter objects, including dishes, plates, handles for jugs and decorative roundels of various kinds. Here, as at Camerton, there can be little doubt that the pewter industry had grown to be an essential part of the subsistence economy.

Marketing the products would have provided no problem, the craftsmen or their employers needing to undertake only a short journey into Bath to find a ready market among the visitors and merchants. Some may have sold their products in bulk to middlemen for distribution from secondary markets in the other towns of the provinces, others would have disposed of individual pieces or sets to the agents of neighbouring landowners who came into Bath to purchase their day-to-day needs. It may be that one craftsman dedicated part of his stock to the presiding deity and threw it into the sacred spring, where it sank to the bottom, some pieces being washed out into the culvert, to be found by excavators 1500 years later.

Such, then, are some of the activities in which the inhabitants of Aquae Sulis and its neighbourhood would have been engaged in the Roman period. Indeed, there would have been very little difference between Bath of the fourth century and the town as late as the seventeenth century. In size, population and economic basis there are many points of close similarity.

Cemeteries

Having discussed the people and their lives, we must briefly consider them in their death. Large numbers of Roman burials have come to light over the years from the neighbourhood of the town, but practically without exception the discoveries were made accidentally and recording, where any was attempted at all, is inadequate. Nevertheless, it is possible to obtain a general impression of the burial practices of the inhabitants.

The earliest burials, dating to the first and second centuries, were cremations, the bones being placed in urns and buried, often with smaller pots of finer quality containing offerings of food to sustain the spirit on its journey to the other world. The poorer cremations would probably have been marked by a simple wooden or stone marker, while the richer burials would have been located by inscribed tombstones of the type we have already considered. The tombstone of Julius Vitalis (see **89**), the armourer of the Twentieth Legion, for example, was found in 1708 close to two simple cinerary urns, one presumably containing the food, the other Vitalis himself. Generally speaking, the richer the occupant the more ostentatious the tomb.

Several of the tombs were adorned with sculptures of considerable merit. From the cemetery

95 *Colossal head of a woman found at Walcot, whose hair is set in a manner fashionable in Rome in the late first century AD. Possibly a tomb sculpture.*

(**95**). Presumably the head once adorned her tomb. Another head, of the theatrical mask of Tragedy (**96**), must also have come from a tomb. Three tomb reliefs are also known. One, found

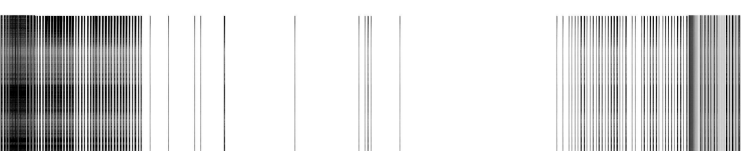

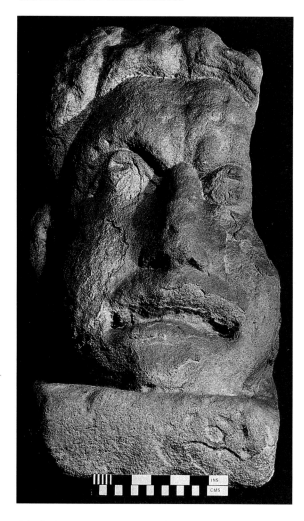

97 *Tombstone of a man from the Fosseway cemetery.*

96 *Sculptured theatrical mask found at Walcot: probably a tomb relief.*

from his belt. A second relief, found at the same time, shows a man with hands folded across his body, probably holding a scroll (**98**); he wears a toga and his hair is brushed forward and cut short. Both depict prominent citizens, men of wealth and status who indulged in Roman manners and dress, and who might well have been decurions. The third relief, which probably comes from a tomb, was dug up in London Road in Walcot in 1860. Though only a small piece, it shows a brilliant rendering of a lion carrying a deer across its back (**99**). It is one of the most accomplished sculptures from Roman Britain.

Fragmentary though our knowledge of the funerary monuments of Bath is, the surviving pieces give a reasonably balanced picture of what it was like to travel north from the town along the Fosseway in the second century. It must have been very similar to an elongated Victorian churchyard with its range of simple markers, inscribed headstones and elaborate family vaults.

Several times mention has been made of the fact that fragments of funerary monuments were built into the city wall. This raises the interesting question of when this was done. Was the early cemetery largely dismantled when the walls were built, possibly in the third century, and the monuments used as rubble, or were the Roman stones used to patch the existing wall in late Saxon or medieval times? The use of funerary monuments as ballast in town walls is certainly well attested in Gaul during the third century and some of the bastions of London incorporate reused stone of this kind, but there is now some doubt as to whether they are fourth century, as originally supposed, or later. Thus while it is an attractive possibility that the old cemetery along the Fosseway was dismantled for use in the construction of the Roman town wall, without further excavation, which is not at the moment possible, the question must remain open.

The change-over from cremation to inhumation took place gradually throughout the third century, providing incidentally a great boost for the local stone industry which was now required to produce large quantities of stone sarcophagi for those who could afford them. The less

wealthy were buried in simple wooden coffins while occasionally more expensive lead lining was used, as in the case of the coffin found at Bathwick in 1819. The early records of the discoveries of Roman inhumations give some idea of the rituals involved and the beliefs of the people. Often the dead were provided with coins to pay Charon to ferry the soul across the River

98 *Tombstone of a man from the Fosseway cemetery.*

99 *Tomb relief showing a lion carrying a young deer across its back; from London Road, Walcot. Height 40cm (16in)*

Styx; sometimes, for example with one of the Combe Down burials, the coin was placed on the lips of the departed. Generally, grave-goods were not common, but dress-pins, rings and brooches show that the bodies were clothed, while the discovery of hobnails at the feet implies that often people were buried in their boots. Occasionally more exotic offerings were placed in the graves, as in the burial found near Sydney Buildings which included a bronze box 'which opened with a spring' containing eight bronze coins.

On the whole the bodies were laid on their backs in various orientations, but examples are known from the Bath area where the dead were laid face-downwards in their coffins, presumably for some religious reason. Two burials, found at Bathwick Hill in 1861, are of particular interest. Both bodies were placed in stone coffins, one packed in fine white sand, the other in a coarser sand. The first coffin contained a young woman, the second a child of fourteen or fifteen years. This may well be an example of an attempt at preserving the body from decay in the same way that gypsum was used for this purpose in York. Tiny pieces of fabric were said to have been found preserved in the sand, together with particles of a bituminous material which might hint at some form of embalming. The sand was unfortunately not analysed, but fine white sand is sometimes deposited by the spring and it may be that such a deposit was considered to have preservative qualities. These Bathwick Hill burials provide an interesting insight into the aspirations of the inhabitants of the town and their hopes of a happy afterlife.

7

The end

The end came to different parts of the town at different times. First to suffer were the baths and the temple, which together lay in a slight hollow in the centre of the settlement around the main spring. It seems that throughout the third and fourth centuries the sea-level had been rising and with it the general water-table of the inland areas, causing a series of floods of gradually increasing severity. It was to counteract the flooding of the hypocausts that the levels of the basement floors were raised late in the development of the baths, but as time went on even the new floors suffered sporadic submersion and thick layers of grey and black mud were deposited by the flood waters between the *pilae* of the hypocausts. The discovery of these silts raised the question of whether or not it was the spring water that was causing the damage. However, a detailed chemical analysis established beyond doubt that the muds were the result of flood waters from the River Avon backing up along the drains at times when the river was in full spate. The sediment was gradually precipitated from the standing water, which eventually receded leaving the mud to dry. Then the river would again flood and the process would begin once more. Exactly the same problems of flooding still exist today. Though modern river controls are reducing the frequency of flooding, until quite recently each year, often several times a

water to recede. It must have meant periods of days or even weeks when the establishment would have been out of use. As the economic and political stability of the province began to shake, the impetus, or the financial ability, to clear out the mud and repair the flood damage would have weakened until at one particular point in time it was decided to abandon the establishment altogether. But perhaps this is putting it too strongly – it might be more accurate to say that the decision to reopen the baths failed to be taken. The mud remained and the end had begun.

One of the most glaring omissions of the Victorian excavations was their virtual lack of interest in the mud and soil which choked the baths. To the excavators it was rubbish to be removed as soon as possible. Irvine attempted to record some archaeological sections, but by the time most of the work was being undertaken he had left Bath and there was no one of his calibre to take over. In consequence there is practically nothing to be said of the processes involved in the gradual destruction of the building. On the other hand the adjacent temple area, much of which escaped Victorian clearance, still retains its overburden of silt and rubble to a depth of 2m (6½ft).

The excavations of 1965–8 and 1981–3 allowed these fascinating layers to be examined in detail: incorporated in the soil was the entire story of the temple precinct from the moment the

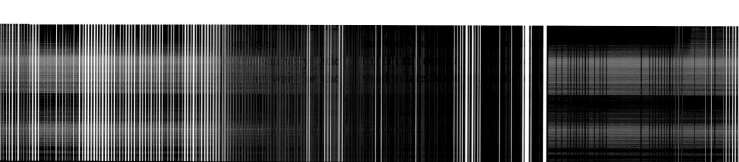

100 *The temple precinct during excavation. Beyond the horizontal rod scale the thick layer of soil represents successive floors and mud accumulations reflecting continuous use. The latest is sealed by the collapse of the superstructure.*

(6½ft) of soil representing 700 years of neglect and change (**100**). For ease of discussion we have divided the late sequence into four periods – periods 5–8 (periods 1–4 being the earlier building phases of the temple, see Chapter 3). During period 5 we see the attempts of the late or sub-Roman population to keep the old building in use but the Roman drainage system had broken down and the low-lying area of the inner precinct around the altar seems to have become susceptible to periodic flooding. At any event thick black soil began to accumulate. Periodically the ground surface was consolidated with a tip of rubble or a spread of poor-quality concrete but still the waterlogging occurred and more soil and silt accumulated until the deposit had grown to a depth of 60cm (24in). Fortunately some of the pollen of the locally growing plants became incorporated in the mud and because of its semi-waterlogged condition a reasonable sample has survived. Very common were grains of various grasses and the usual garden weeds such as the dandelion family (*Liguliflorae*), together with pollen from cereals and the weeds of cultivation which characterize farmed land, plants such as ribwort plantain. All these probably indicate what was being grown in the general locality rather than the specific spot in the centre of the town. Other plants more related to the actual marsh were the sedges, reedmace and the gentians. Mosses, ferns and bracken were also represented, all typical of marshy conditions which by this time must have lain within and around the buildings. While the waterlogging prevailed in the low-lying parts around the baths and temple, the rest of the town, unaffected by the flooding, continued to be inhabited, its rubbish, including pottery and animal bones, now being tipped into the precinct area.

The last repaving was carried out on a more substantial scale. The portico north of the reservoir and part of the area of the precinct to the north was paved with close-set limestone slabs robbed from standing Roman buildings. The niched quadrangular monument (above, p. 59) was used in this way and so was the fine relief of Diana's hound (see **44**), but even more interesting was the discovery of one of the blocks of the temple pediment, used upside-down as paving, in the excavation of 1982. It now seems highly likely that the other pediment blocks, found in 1790, had also been used in this way but since their backs were sawn off and discarded at the time of discovery, it is no longer possible to see if they, like the 1982 block, were worn.

The reuse of sculptured monuments as paving raises many interesting questions: was this done deliberately as an act of desecration and if so when and by whom? It was at about this time that the altar was dismantled and its corners pushed over. Together the evidence is suggestive of some conscious process designed to remove the iconography of the pagan religion. One possible

The new paving, which marks the last constructional phase of period 5, remained in active use for some while, becoming very worn. All this time the temple buildings were still standing. Then, in period 6, the superstructure of the portico and possibly part of the reservoir enclosure collapsed, or was pushed over, creating a scree of massive stone blocks mixed up with slabs of concrete and shattered tiles from the vaults (**101**). Whether or not the collapse was deliberately contrived, it is clear that the inhabitants raked through the rubble to remove the iron clamps and their lead settings, which had once held the structure together, leaving the thick layer of rubble to serve as a convenient foundation for subsequent floors. Dating is difficult but by this time we must be in the eighth or ninth century. Already, in the centre of the precinct where the soil was deeper and less rubbly, a cemetery was beginning to develop marking the beginning of a long period of burial which came to an end in the sixteenth century with the Dissolution.

While we can be specific about the inner precinct, how the entire complex – the baths, spring and temple – fared we can only guess.

After the roofs had fallen in, the old monument must have formed a dramatic and rather sad sight, with its columns, piers and probably its entablatures standing in ruins, projecting gauntly from the engulfing marsh. Towards the centre would have been the bubbling, steaming spring, the waters swirling away from the sources and lapping against fallen and standing masonry alike, leaving a thick crust of bright red iron oxide stain on everything. Away from the source would have been lagoons of still, black water giving way to drier land upon which reeds, bracken and small trees such as willow and alder grew, providing homes for wildfowl like the coot or teal, whose egg was found in the old excavations, and for innumerable wild animals. In fact much of the centre of the town would have reverted to the state in which the Roman engineers found it

which constantly springs to mind is of a stage set for a willowy Victorian romance – slightly ominous grey architecture seen against wispy blue-green light. It was into this setting that the early Christian community was injected.

The drama of the ruins was certainly not lost upon those who were able to observe them at first hand. An Anglo-Saxon poem called 'The

Ruin', written in the eighth century quite possibly by a monk, almost certainly describes the scene in Bath as it then was:

Wondrous is this masonry, shattered by the Fates. The fortifications have given way, the buildings raised by giants are crumbling. The roofs have collapsed; the towers are in ruins. ... There is rime on the mortar. The walls are rent and broken away, and have fallen undermined by age. The owners and builders are perished and gone, and have been held fast in

101 *The temple precinct. The tumbled mass of the portico in front of the reservoir enclosure is seen here just as it fell in the Saxon period.*

the earth's embrace, the ruthless clutch of the grave, while a hundred generations of mankind have passed away. Red of hue and hoary with lichen this wall has outlasted kingdom after kingdom, standing unmoved by storms. The lofty arch has fallen.... Resolute in spirit he marvellously clamped the foundations of the walls with ties. There were splendid palaces and many halls with water flowing through them; a wealth of gables towered aloft... .

And so these courts lie desolate, and the framework of the dome with its red arches sheds its tiles ... where of old many a warrior, joyous hearted and radiant with gold, shone resplendent in the harness of battle, proud and flushed with wine. He gazed upon the treasure, the silver, the precious stones, upon wealth, riches and pearls, upon this splendid citadel of a broad domain. There stood courts of stone, and a stream gushed forth in rippling floods of hot water. The wall enfolded within its bright bosom the whole place which contained the hot flood of the baths... . (N. Kershaw, *Anglo-Saxon and Norse Poems*, Cambridge University Press, 1922)

All the elements described by the poet are supported with remarkable precision by the archaeological evidence. Here is, without doubt, a dramatic eyewitness account of the Roman town in its death-throes. By the eighth century enough of the superstructure, less the vaults, was still standing to be intelligible to the Anglo-Saxon poet, but by the eleventh century most of the old structure had probably disappeared, perhaps as the result of late Saxon builders removing suitable stone for reuse in the building programmes that were being undertaken at this time.

While it is true to say that the baths and temple had ceased to function in the manner for which they were built after the beginning of the

continued to be occupied for a considerable period of time after the nominal end of Roman Britain in 410 and there is no reason to suppose that this was atypical. Town life in some form or another must have continued until, by 973, Bath had emerged as a town important enough to stage the coronation of King Edgar.

The processes which brought about the decline and re-emergence can be reconstructed, if only in broad outline, partly on the evidence from Bath itself and partly on analogy with sites in other parts of the country. In general terms the early fourth century was a period of prosperity for the towns and villa-owners, and even the peasant classes seem to have shared in the general affluence. Specialist schools of mosaicists could now be supported on the patronage offered by the rich, many of whom, like the owner of the Newton-St-Loe villa, were able to employ a team, probably based on Cirencester, whose speciality was the design and laying of figured mosaics depicting the Orpheus legend. But gradually, as the middle of the century approached, signs of the impending breakdown began to become noticeable. Manpower was in short supply, reflecting a decline in the birth-rate, and consequently restrictive laws were passed to prevent the free movement of workers from one job to another. Tax burdens and the expensive responsibilities of public service were also making their effect felt in most areas, particularly the urban centres, but in spite of all this there was a sustained affluence which showed itself in the expensive alterations to the baths which continued to be made throughout the fourth century.

More serious than the purely economic factors were the threats from barbarian raiders, particularly the Picts and the Scots, which grew in their intensity until finally, in 367, the great 'Barbarian Conspiracy' launched a series of concerted raids on Britain. Picts, Scots, Franks, Saxons, Attocotti and Irish, aided by a disgruntled peasantry and no intention of military take-over or settlement. This is why when, two years later, Count Theodosius landed at Richborough with his army, he was unopposed, and by means of coercion and bribery, was able to restore the situation to order without undue delay.

The restoration which Theodosius engineered was thorough. The frontiers of both land and sea were put into order again by regarrisoning Hadrian's Wall and by reorganizing, with extensions, the so-called Saxon Shore defences. The administrative machinery was supported and strengthened when necessary and, apparently for the first time, the towns were turned into strongly fortified bases from which a militia could spring into action if needed. The evidence for this is twofold: many of the towns with early third-century walls were strengthened at about this time by the addition of forward-projecting bastions fronted by a wide flat-bottomed ditch, the bastions to support war machines such as ballistae and catapults, the ditch to keep any would-be attackers within the optimum killing range. Where towns or settlements were not already walled, such as Mildenhall, some kilometres east of Bath, a wall complete with attached bastions was built afresh. Although the dating evidence for each individual site is often vague, if it is correct to assume that these new works were all part of a unified scheme, the best context consistent with the available archaeological facts would be the Theodosian restoration. The second interesting piece of evidence is the occurrence of a distinct class of military fittings, usually of bronze, from forts and towns in southern Britain. It has been shown that these are of Germanic inspiration and may represent equipment used either by the soldiers brought to Britain by Theodosius or by mercenaries from north Europe imported for the purpose of defending the towns. However this material is interpreted, its very existence, together with the modified defences, leaves little doubt that many of the towns had now become strongly fortified entities protected by resident troops.

It is not yet possible to say how Bath fitted into this pattern, although the uncertainty about the date of the town wall leaves open the possibility that it was not built until the late fourth century. Nor is it known whether the town was ever provided with bastions. The earliest town map dating to about 1570, shows a series of bastions in some detail attached at intervals to all sides of the circuit, but it is very diagrammatic and the total absence of bastions on any of the later town maps, even that produced only forty years later by Speed, is puzzling. Either the early cartographer allowed himself considerable artistic licence or the defences had been completely modified during the Elizabethan period. It seems very unlikely, however, that a town in such a strategic position would have been left unprotected while others on lesser sites were now defended.

The events of 369 and the immediately following years were the last time that the central Roman government concerned itself directly with the affairs of the province. Thereafter Britain took care of itself by appointing a series of military commanders of varying degrees of competence, whose one ambition seems to have been to win a major battle on the Continent, in theory to protect Britain but usually to make a bid for the throne. To this end one army after another was amassed in the province only to be carried off to fight abroad, eventually to fail and be dispersed. By 409 there can hardly have been more than a handful of fighting men left. The countryside was in a state of turmoil, certain sectors of the community – quite possibly the peasants – having rebelled against the administrators and thrown them out, setting up 'a state of their own' as the writer Zosimus says. Then in 410 the final blow came: the Emperor Honorius, replying to a letter asking for help, firmly told the towns to look after their own defences. Britain was now on its own.

What followed is obscure but one thing stands out: many of the towns did survive as working entities. Even so, with government now fragmented and in the hands of tyrants and with the complex economic system of the Roman period in ruins, forcing society back into a state of bartering, the vitality of the cities was wasted. At best the surviving urban communities should be regarded as parasites on the carcass of the Roman achievement.

The sub-Roman leaders were faced with the threat of attack from most of the old enemies whom Theodosius had driven away in 369. A tradition says that two opposed policies were favoured in the fifth century. Ambrosius wished to renew ties with the Roman armies who were still struggling on the Continent, while Vortigern supported the idea of continuing to bring in Saxon mercenaries, settling them in coastal regions as a kind of yeomanry to protect the land from amphibious raiders. To begin with Vortigern's policies prevailed but not without opposition, which caused him to build up his mercenary support. In about 442 the inevitable happened, the Saxon settlers rebelled and swept across the south and east in a series of plundering raids in which their relations from the homeland soon joined. Gildas, writing about a hundred years after, describes the event in vivid if rather exaggerated terms:

> For the fire of vengeance, justly kindled by former crimes, spread from sea to sea, fed by the hands of our foes in the east, and did not cease, until, destroying the neighbouring towns and lands, it reached the other side of the island, and dipped its red and savage tongue in the western ocean... . So that all the columns were levelled with the ground by the frequent strokes of the battering ram, all the husbandmen routed, together with their bishops, priests, and people, whilst the sword gleamed, and the flames crackled around them on every side. Lamentable to behold, in the midst of the streets lay the tops of lofty towers, tumbled to the ground, stones of high walls, holy altars, fragments of human bodies, covered with livid clots of coagulated blood, looking as if they had been squeezed together in a wine-press; and with no chance of being buried save in the ruins

Needless to say, the rebellion marked the end of Vortigern's pro-Saxon policy and with the east of Britain now under Saxon domination the centre of the resistance moved to the west.

Whether the raiders reached the neighbourhood of Bath it is impossible to say. There are some signs of disorder in the area, such as the burning down of the villa at Box and the bodies tipped down the well of the North Wraxall villa, but both of these events probably belonged to earlier troubles. In Bath itself the severed head of the girl thrown into the oven of the house in Abbeygate Street could well belong to the 440s, but precise dating is entirely lacking. However far the war bands had penetrated, they seem soon to have returned to the eastern areas and left the west to the control of the shadowy sub-Roman war leaders such as Ambrosius and Arthur. Soon after the rebellion had subsided, in about 446, an appeal for help was made to the Roman general Aetius: 'the Barbarians drive us to the sea, the sea drives us to the Barbarians. Between the two means of death we are either slaughtered or drowned.' Another overstatement and one, it seems, to which there was no response.

The next fifty years saw a period of raids and battles but the west maintained successful independence, winning a number of cavalry victories over their Saxon opponents, culminating in the famous victory at Mount Badon in about AD 500. After this, Gildas could speak of a time of security but, he goes on, 'neither to this day are the cities of our country inhabited as before but being forsaken and overthrown, still lie desolate'.

By the middle of the sixth century the Saxon advance had gained a new impetus and eventually in 577 at the battle of Dyrham in the Cotswolds, 10km (6 miles) north of Bath, the Saxons won a decisive victory, gaining the three towns of Bath, Cirencester and Gloucester. That the towns are mentioned at all in the *Anglo-Saxon Chronicle* is some indication that they were con-

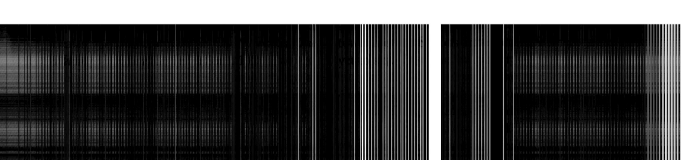

Glossary

ambulatory a covered walk around the outside of a building

apodyterium an undressing room

architrave horizontal member immediately above a row of columns

blind arcading an arcade set against a blank wall

caldarium the hot room in a bathing establishment

cella principal room of a temple usually containing the cult statue and sacred objects.

colonnade row of columns

cornice uppermost member of the entablature

entablature the horizontal members (architrave, frieze and cornice) above a row of columns

exedra (pl. *exedrae*) open bay or recess in a wall

ex-voto offering made to a deity

frieze part of the entablature (between the architrave and cornice) above a row of columns

frigidarium cold room in a bathing establishment

laconicum a room of hot, dry heat in a bathing establishment

lunette curve-topped opening often in the end of a vaulted roof

pediment the triangular gable end of a temple above the front columns

pilae square tiles set one upon another to form pillars to support the floors of hypocausts

portico porch area

pronaos porch in front of the cella of a temple

prostyle structure having a projecting façade supported on columns

pseudoperipteral half columns attached to the external wall of a building

quadrifrons monument with two arched passages set at right angles

stylobate stone foundation blocks for a colonnade

tepidarium the warm room in a bath suite

tholos circular building, often a temple

Places to visit

This is easy advice to provide! The monuments and remains of Roman Bath are presented together in the Pump Room and Roman Baths complex in the centre of the city where it is possible to explore at leisure much of the Roman thermal establishment and the temple precinct as well as to see all the important Roman sculpture and small finds from the city. To be allowed to walk freely on the Roman pavements is a memorable privilege.

Elsewhere in the town there is little of Roman interest to be seen except for glimpses of the medieval city wall which probably follows its Roman predecessor.

Bath has, of course, many attractions and takes many days to explore, even superficially. Not to be missed are the **Abbey Heritage Vaults** (entrance just south of the abbey transept) where Saxon and medieval finds are well displayed, and the **Building of Bath Museum** in the Huntington Centre, The Paragon, which provides a fascinating insight into the practicalities of building the eighteenth- and nineteenth-century city.

Further reading

Roman Bath is well served in the published literature. In the second edition of *Roman Bath Discovered* (1984), pp. 223–8, I have provided a full bibliography of both the antiquarian literature and detailed papers published in journals. The same volume includes a rather more extended account of the history of archaeological discovery within the city than it has been possible to offer in the present book.

Recent excavations

Archaeology in Bath: 1976–1985 P. Davenport (ed.) (Oxford 1991)

Excavations in Bath: 1950–1975 B. Cunliffe (ed.) (Bath 1979)

Roman Bath B. Cunliffe (London 1969)

The Temple of Sulis Minerva at Bath volume 1: *The Site* B. Cunliffe and P. Davenport (Oxford 1985)

The Temple of Sulis Minerva at Bath volume 2: *The Finds from the Sacred Spring* B. Cunliffe (ed.) (Oxford 1988)

General accounts of Bath and the Roman Baths

The City of Bath B. Cunliffe (Gloucester 1986)

The Roman Baths: A view over 2000 years B. Cunliffe (Bath 1993)

General background to Roman Britain and its religion

Britannia: A history of Roman Britain S.S. Frere (London: 3rd edn 1987)

Religion in Roman Britain M. Henig (London 1984)

Roman Britain P. Salway (Oxford 1981)

The Small Towns of Roman Britain J. Wacher and B. Burnham (London 1990)

Index

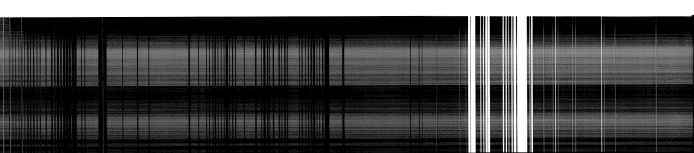